RECOVERING
FROM RACISM

RECOVERING FROM RACISM

CITY MINISTRY IN A "POST-RACIAL" AMERICA

LARRY LLOYD

foreward by WILLIAM PANNELL &
post script by JOHN PERKINS

ENGAGE
FAITH
P R E S S

For permission requests, please address
Engage Faith Publishing
7300 West Joy Road
Dexter, Michigan 48130

Published 2014 by Engage Faith Publishing
Printed in the United States of America

18 17 16 15 14   1 2 3 4 5

ISBN 978-1-936672-86-8

Library of Congress Control Number: 2014951630

Contents

Foreword

by Dr. William Pannell

Emeritus Professor of Preaching

I have waited a long time for this book. I have known the author for many years, although when he appeared in my office at the seminary neither of us had any idea that he would write a book about ministry in his home town. Not many seminary graduates return home for their life's work, but then Larry never really left. Memphis is in his DNA. He married Becky there, they raised their children there, struggled against the demons of church and society there. This is really their story and Dr. Lloyd writes it just like he lives it; what you read is what he is, and how he thinks.

This story is important because for more than a century evangelicals have largely been absent from the struggle for justice and community development. It has meant that they have been cut off from the earlier labors of men and women who pioneered ministries in the name of the Kingdom. These leaders were in the forefront of attempts to flesh out the meaning of the Gospel in urban centers where injustice and discrimination prevailed. One thinks of the early Methodists in England, the "army" led by William and Catherine Booth, or those gutsy women who led the Women's Christian Temperance Union, Frances E. Willard, and Anna Howard Shaw; Walter Rauschenbusch, Washington Gladden and others whose work gave rise to the so-called "social gospel," the Catholic Workers movement and Dorothy Day. Being severed from this rich tradition of urban work has meant that evangelicals failed to grasp the significance of Jesus' words to his disciples when he told them that laboring in His Father's world was a matter of continuity. "Others have labored', he said, 'and you have entered into their labors." It has meant also that evangelicals have severed themselves from the heartbeat of one of their most cherished evangelists. The Apostle Paul, in Wayne Meeks fine writing, "was a city person. The city breathes through his writings." What is often forgotten is the significance of cities in the ministry of the early church. One only needs read the captions of the Epistles to realize that much of the early church's life was spent in bringing the Gospel to cities.

It was the emergence of cities as centers of American social, economic and political life that gave birth to new concerns about justice. These earlier pioneers did make a difference. No less an urban "evangelist" than Martin L. King Jr. admitted that the work of Rauschenbusch was seminal in the shaping of his thinking regarding social issues. "Although my main interest was in the field of theology and philosophy, I spent a great deal of time reading the works of the great social philosophers. I came early to the works of Walter Rauschenbusch's Christianity and the Social Crisis which left an indelible imprint on my thinking by giving me a theological basis for the social concern which had already grown up in me as a result of my early experiences." (Stride Toward Freedom, Harper and Row, 1958, Pg. 91) The crisis about which the Baptist philosopher-preachers labored was the plight of people trapped by injustice in American cities.

But in recent years there has been a movement of sorts among a newer generation of evangelicals called to serve the Kingdom in American cities. Today many of them gather under the umbrella of the Christian Community Development Association and work from centers as diverse as New York City, Pittsburgh, Atlanta, Chicago, Los Angeles, and of course Memphis. I cite these ministries because they grew out of white evangelical leadership led, in no small part, by none other than the African American social activist John Perkins of Jackson, Mississippi. But somehow Memphis is different, and the difference is found in its leadership, and especially the founder of The Memphis Leadership Foundation. Through this work the city is not the same as when the young Larry Lloyd began his pilgrimage toward justice. His is the story of why his city is different in key areas of its life.

Oh, and there is this. Some ninety years ago a baby girl was born in the black community in Memphis. She lived near Booker T. Washington High School and years later became one of its graduates. Upon graduation, she left Memphis, and eventually settled in Detroit where she became a disciple of Jesus and married a preacher. I'm glad she did and my wife will really enjoy this story.

Chapter 1
Black Memphis
1968

*For he makes his sun rise on the evil and on the good, and
sends rain on the just and on the unjust.*

—Matthew 5:45, ESV

*Jesus was a garbage collector too. Praise His Name! He went
about the world trying to clean up garbage. People's lives were
full of garbage, still are, all kinds of garbage: hatred, spite,
envy, vanity, violence, despair. They fight and kill each other
in wars all over the world for reasons so old they can't even
remember them. Jesus tried His best to destroy the garbage,
but like our dearly departed, He also lost His life.*

—Reverend Moore, in "I Am A Man" by Oyamo

It all started with rain.

On Tuesday, February 1, 1968, in Memphis, Tennessee, two
garbage men—that's what they were called back then—sat
inside the rear of a truck to wait out a storm. While huddled
in the only shelter available to them, a switch accidentally
flipped, and the men were crushed to death in the churning
maw of the compactor.

The truth is, the tragedy of that February day was just one

drop in an already full bucket of sorrow that had been raining on Memphis for a long time. Sanitation workers were among the lowest paid of city employees, with few, if any, benefits. The men carried metal tubs that leaked garbage onto their shoulders as they hauled trash from the backs of houses to the trucks on the street. The city did not provide them with gloves, uniforms, or a place to shower. The workers, nearly all black, formed a union and tried more than once to get Memphis to officially recognize them, to no avail. It was as if they didn't exist. Like the garbage they carried away from every home in town, they were a fact of life best left unnoticed. And when the families of the two dead men asked for compensation, they were refused. Ignored.

A few days later, it rained again. Twenty-two sewer workers were sent home without pay. That's when the African American community in Memphis finally said enough is enough. A switch flipped. This time, it was no accident. Before it was all over, everyone knew what it was to be crushed.[1]

Memphis as Microcosm

We are all familiar with the drama of the civil rights movement. It is a broad, sweeping epoch in our country's history, with all the attendant elements of defeat and victory, villains and champions, embarrassment and pride, death and life, rain and sunshine. In the space of less than three months, Memphis lived it all. In the space of less than three months, Memphis blacks took on a city that was indifferent, a mayor who refused to listen, and the stinking injustice of one of its most necessary industries. And won. But not without paying a heavy price before it was all over. Memphis paid a price… and still does.

1   http://www.apwu.org/laborhistory/05-1_memphissanitationworkers/05-1_memphissanitationworkers.htm

The Memphis Sanitation Workers' Strike began just twelve days after the accident that killed those two men. Only 200 of the city's 1,300 sanitation workers remained on the job. Only 38 of its 180 trucks rolled on the city streets. Mayor Henry Loeb declared the strike illegal and ordered the men back to work.[2] Unlike Rosa Parks' refusal to move on a Montgomery bus or the quiet presence of four students at a segregated lunch counter in Greensboro, these men gave Memphis more to contend with than their protests: within two days 10,000 tons of garbage piled up all over the city.[3] Something had been rotten in Memphis for decades, and it was time for everyone to smell it.

As the garbage piled higher and higher, the conflict escalated. Black ministers and leaders formed a citywide organization to support the strike. They put on an eight-hour gospel-singing marathon at the Mason Temple to raise money for the strikers. In response, the city obtained a court injunction to keep the union from staging demonstrations or picketing. The strike eventually gained the attention of national leaders, including Martin Luther King Jr., International Union officials, the NAACP, African American ministers in the community, State Senator Frank White, AFL-CIO President George Meany, and President Lyndon Johnson himself, all of whom made overtures to Mayor Loeb, offering to help negotiate a peaceful settlement. He rejected them all. During a march led by Dr. King, police moved into crowds with nightsticks, mace, tear gas, and gunfire. A sixteen-year-old boy, Larry Payne, was shot to death as police arrested 280 protestors.[4] About

---

2   http://www.afscme.org/union/history/mlk/1968-afscme-memphis-sanitation-workers-strike-chronology

3   Ibid.

4   Michael K. Honey, *Going Down Jericho Road: The Memphis Strike, Martin Luther King's Last Campaign* (New York: W. W. Norton and Company, 2008), 360.

sixty people were injured, mostly blacks. At this point in the conflict, 4,000 National Guardsmen moved in on Memphis.[5] And the garbage piled higher and higher.

I Am A Man

Human dignity. Our country is founded upon it. We not only welcome those who seek dignity and freedom, our Statue of Liberty stands at New York Harbor and beckons them: "Give me your tired, your poor, your huddled masses yearning to breathe free, the wretched refuse of your teeming shore." We champion those who rise above their circumstances and become something. Kudos to those who grab their piece of the American dream, the self-made, the conquerors. Human dignity, we applaud it. We cheer for those who display it, those who prove it. "The pursuit of happiness" is every person's inalienable right, isn't it? Unless we don't consider that person human.

The men who marched in the Sanitation Workers' Strike wore placards that proclaimed: "I Am A Man." Just one generation ago, it was necessary in parts of our country for some human beings to advertise their own humanity. That's what our record of slavery, Jim Crow, segregation, and racism had wrought upon the African American community in our Southern cities, indeed, throughout America. Reverend James Lawson, a Memphis minister and head of the strike committee, observed, "At the heart of racism is the idea that a man is not a man."[6] *This* was the focal point of the strike. Men called upon the city to treat them as men. This was the message that drew Martin Luther King Jr., along with other

---

5   http://www.afscme.org/about/1548.cfm

6   Townsend Davis, Weary Feet, Rested Souls: A Guided History of the Civil Rights Movement (New York: W. W. Norton and Company, 1999), 365.

leaders of the civil rights movement, to join the struggle in Memphis.

On April 3, with the strike and the city still unsettled, Dr. King delivered his "I've Been to the Mountaintop" address to a crowd at Bishop Charles Mason Temple:

> *We are saying that we are determined to be men. We are determined to be people. (Yeah) We are saying [Applause], we are saying that we are God's children. (Yeah) [Applause] And if we are God's children, we don't have to live like we are forced to live.*[7]

The next day, Dr. King was assassinated as he stood on the balcony of his room at the Lorraine Motel. Four days later, Mrs. King and national leaders led a memorial march through downtown Memphis in honor of her husband and in support of the strike. On **Tuesday, April 16,** union leaders announced that an agreement had been reached.[8] The strikers voted to accept it. The strike was over.

Racism/rac-ism/noun:
A belief that race is the primary determinant of human traits and capacities and that racial differences produce an inherent superiority of a particular race (Merriam-Webster)

Part of remembering is bringing the memories into focus, defining their shape and substance. When the recollections become lucid, only then can we grapple with the ideas that formed them. At the end of each chapter, I'll attempt to do just that: to identify and describe words like racism, paternalism,

---

7   http://www.americanrhetoric.com/speeches/mlkivebeentothemoun-taintop.htm

8   Honey, *Going Down Jericho Road*, 496.

and privilege, those words we'd like to scrub from our vocabularies and our lives. After all, don't we live in a post-racial America? Aren't racism and segregation things of the past? I'll also bring clarity to the terms we embrace, like diversity, justice, and righteousness.

Looking Back

History always begs questions. Always. What really happened and why? What effect did those happenings have on life as we know it today? Where did the real action take place? And who was there?

The questions that haunt me about Memphis in 1968 have proven to shape the rest of my life. I was sixteen and confused, often oblivious. I didn't ask the questions then. But, it wasn't too long before I did. I asked them at first because I had my own personal answers to give. I keep asking because the injustice that plagued Memphis and America then plagues us still. No, it doesn't look the same. Yes, things are better. But questions must be asked to understand what part I, and those like me, played in Memphis's history, in America's history. And to understand what role we must play now.

Where was I? I grew up in Memphis. But that doesn't really answer the question. "Where was I?" is a much bigger question than that. That's because I represent an entire part of Memphis that was mostly absent during the strike of 1968. Our garbage piled up in our backyards just like everyone else's. We were there. But, in almost every sense but physically, we were absent. Morally, socially, and spiritually: we never showed up. Our absence provokes the real question:

Where was the white church? The "evangelical, conservative" church? Where were we and where are we now?

Dr. King commended the pastors who were present at the rally the day before his death. Among African American pastors was a sprinkling of so-called "liberal" white pastors and some rabbis who participated in the civil rights movement. The white evangelical church was largely absent. It was the African American ministers who led the charge in Memphis, and Dr. King appreciated that:

> *Who is it that is supposed to articulate the longings and aspirations of the people more than the preacher? Somewhere the preacher must have a kind of fire shut up in his bones (Yes), and whenever injustice is around he must tell it. Somehow the preacher must be an Amos, who said, "When God Speaks, who can but prophesy?" (Yes) Again with Amos, "Let justice roll down like waters and righteousness like a mighty stream." (Yes) Somehow the preacher must say with Jesus, "The spirit of the Lord is upon me (Yes), because He hath anointed me (Yes), and He's anointed me to deal with the problems of the poor.[9]"*

Where was the white evangelical church? Where were the brothers and sisters in the faith of these courageous pastors? Not just on the sidelines. They were often applauding the decision of the mayor who would underscore the bold line that already existed between black and white. They were decrying the sit-ins, the Freedom Rides, the peaceful demonstrations, the cry for equality. They were complaining, at the same time, about not having "good help" available these days. They were ignorant, willingly blind it seems, of the conditions under which these men worked who picked up our garbage, men who had served our country at war, fathers and husbands, deacons, preachers and elders in their churches, leaders in their communities. No, ignorant is not quite the right word...more like supportive of white privilege

---

9   http://www.americanrhetoric.com/speeches/mlkivebeentothemountaintop.htm

and black "inferiority." The men who picked up our garbage were invisible to the privileged wealthy white community in which I grew up.

Yes, history leaves behind its share of questions. Big, meaningful, messy questions. And, if there are places where the broader sweep of history intersects with your personal history, the one to which you and only you were an eyewitness, then you can't help but remember it. It becomes etched on your psyche. Just as an entire generation now remembers where they were on September 11, 2001, I remember where I was on the most infamous day of the sanitation workers' strike, the day Martin Luther King Jr. was killed.

I am privileged. I am white. I am the white evangelical church. And I am trying to remember.

Whatcha gonna do?

1. Do you have any personal memories of racism or discrimination based on race? If so, how did they impact you?
2. How prevalent do you believe racism is in your city, neighborhood, school, church...today? What impact does it have?
3. What are the demographics of your church? How does that reflect your community?
4. When I talk about white privilege, how does that sound to you? Is it true? If so, how have you seen it play out in your own history or the history of others you know?

Chapter 2
White Memphis
1968

When I was toting garbage, I knowed every alcoholic in town, da ones live in da shacks and da ones what living high in the big houses. I knowed who was creepin' 'round some back doe on day husband or wife. I knowed who was taking high price drugstore drugs and street drugs... I seed big impo'tent men in dis town beating on soft, little white womens in da back bedrooms. I heard dem womens scream and beg for mercy... One time I pulled a dead baby from the garbage, a little white baby, blood still fresh. Somebody throwed it in the garbage behine a fine mansion. And peepas treat me like I stink. Nothin' stinks worse den the da garbage dat da garbage man leave behine everyday.

—T.O. Jones, in "I Am A Man" by Oyamo

Each of you is on trial today.

—Rev. James Lawson, in a memo
"To All Marchers" on April 8, 1968[10]

...he passed by on the other side.

—Jesus, referring to the priest in the Parable
of the Good Samaritan (Luke 10:31 NIV)

---

10 http://mlk-kpp01.stanford.edu/primarydocuments/680408-010.pdf

I suppose the garbage in our backyard stank to high heaven that early spring of 1968. But I was a teenager, so I didn't notice. And had the strike been in the summer...well, you can only imagine!

The men who usually carried our garbage away with polite stealth every week were marching the streets of Memphis instead. I didn't know it, but there was a mighty struggle going on in my city. Two polarities squared off in the courtrooms and in the streets. One side sought recognition as human beings. The other refused them that dignity.

But I didn't notice.

I was in tenth grade at Central High School. I was white and privileged—the inherent trait of the affluent young—oblivious for the most part. Newly possessed of a driver's license, I didn't have a care in the world. I was free to fixate on that adolescent trifecta: sports, girls, and rock 'n' roll. Trash in our backyard? What did I care?

My Kind of Racism

I grew up in a conservative, upper-class neighborhood in the midtown area of Memphis. Both of my parents were "born again" Christians. That's the term Evangelicals were comfortable with in those days. It was a label that separated the "real" Christians from the "pretenders," or the "liberals" who were considered, at best, lukewarm believers from those who embraced the Bible with a firmer grip.

I was never raised to hate anyone. While many of my friends regularly used derogatory names for African Americans, Jews and Catholics, this was not a part of our household culture. I now see that this was crucial to my developing worldview. Somehow I just knew that this sort of hate language was contrary to my parents' code of ethics. I would later find that it was contrary to the Bible verses I had memorized over the years, too. But I didn't make the connection until years later.

I don't remember my parents ever speaking disparagingly about African Americans. Negro or "colored" was the term used most often in those days. The term "Black" was reserved for the more "radical elements" of the African American community, like the Black Panthers, Stokely Carmichael, or Malcolm X. My parents were fair-minded and deeply committed to Christ. They were removed from the more generalized and overt racism I saw in most people in that "born again" community in which we were entrenched.

I don't remember the sin of racism or bigotry ever preached against from the pulpit in my church, though I suspect it was in others, but those "others" were no doubt the liberals we were constantly being warned about. I don't remember hearing anything about racism or injustice in Sunday school. There may well have been sermons depicting the evils of racism or prejudice, but I seriously doubt it. I don't remember them, nor do I remember ever hearing anyone admonish believers to be involved in the fight against racism. Justice? Never. Well, not quite; we constantly heard that God is just and that sinners are doomed apart from the reconciling work of Jesus Christ who satisfied the justice of God. But that idea of justice was solely spiritual, theological. It never quite made the connection with "social justice" or "loving my neighbor," especially the neighbor who didn't look like me. Racism and its accompanying injustice were simply assumed and acceptable. In fact, as best we knew how, we were benevolent toward African Americans. The term racism, or the concept of racism, was reserved for the hooded KKK and not a part of my vocabulary or thinking. There were two worlds: one was white and privileged and one was black, inferior, and disadvantaged. It's just the way it was. It's how we grew up in Memphis in those days and, as I discovered later, how America grew up, too.

These memories are like the part my family and I played in the rising tide of racial tension that pulsed in Memphis that year: hazy, undefined, distant. The strike impacted us (besides the sanitation workers' strike, Dr. King called for boycotts of some of our most central industries), yet we remained, like most of the privileged white population, relatively and comfortably detached. The struggle could have continued for months without seizing our attention. Sure, we weren't the ones standing in the streets, screaming slurs against the strikers. We weren't bombing African American churches and killing children like they did in Birmingham. Our opinions were benign about the people whose very livelihood hung in the balance. But a chasm of disinterest and disengagement separated us from the African American community. We were simply not involved in their issues. I didn't notice. Few of us did, until something happened that every person born in the 1950s and raised in the 1960s remembers.

On April 4, 1968, as I drove home from baseball practice, I heard the news. Dr. Martin Luther King Jr., had been assassinated in my hometown. That explained the background noise of sirens and helicopters we'd been hearing late that afternoon. King wasn't *my* hero then, but I knew enough about him to know he was the champion of every black person in Memphis. He had a celebrity status—whether it was infamy or nobility depended on your point of view—that reached beyond Memphis and the South. I immediately knew his death deserved my notice. It wasn't long before the reasons for his death did, too.

We like to think of racism as a thing of the distant past: ugly visions of the KKK or white folks hurling words of hatred at black children integrating Little Rock Central. But racism in Memphis called out the heavy artillery. The National Guard sent tanks to Memphis. Those tanks drove between the protestors on the street and the populace on the sidewalks. They rumbled out messages anyone could decipher: "You are dangerous." "We oppose you." "You cannot be trusted." And "We hate you." Who wants to argue with a tank? This kind of racism—the clumsy, loud, obnoxious kind—is easy to watch on TV and dismiss. It's easy to demonize it and, therefore, conclude I am not *this*. I am not a racist.

Maybe that's a good place to start: to refuse to join the ranks of those who throw stones, who yell curses, who, in the end, assassinate their enemies. But that is not a good place to stay.

Bi-Partisan Evil

"When the first wrong was done to the first Indian, I was there. When the first slaver put out for the Congo, I stood on her deck. Am I not in your books and stories and beliefs, from the first settlement on?... 'Tis true the North claims me for a Southerner and the South for a Northerner, but I am neither. I am merely an honest American like yourself—and of the best descent—for, to tell the truth, Mr. Webster, though I don't like to boast of it, my name is older than this country of yours."
—"The Stranger" in *The Devil and Daniel Webster*,
    by Stephen Vincent Benet

Where were we?

From the beginning, I was woven into the fabric of the white, "born again," conservative, Bible-believing, evangelical church. (Sorry for all the adjectives. I'm just making sure I include as many of the descriptors I can remember.) At first I couldn't help it, and later I chose it. If you are my brother or sister, if you are a strand in the vast cloth of the evangelical church, then you know that our history during the civil rights movement in our country was far from exemplary. You know there were churches in the South that, when given the opportunity to open their doors to their black neighbors, refused with a resounding slam of those ornate doors. You know there were Sunday school teachers who marched with the clan, deacons who planted bombs, religious people who lobbied for segregation in the name of their religion. Ask the question, "Where were we?" of this sector and the answers are easy to come by. Those answers have been examined and those offenders excoriated. As well they should be.

But what about the rest of us? Does the scourge of history belong only to those who rode high on the racism bandwagon? Or is there something for which I/*we* are culpable? Perhaps there is.

I have asked the question "Where were we?" and let its echo hang in the air for a while. Even after the response of those who have hatred and violence to get off their chests fades away, the question remains: Where was I? As I said earlier, my memories aren't crystal clear. But I do know this about myself and many like me: I was...

Comfortable
Affluent
Oblivious
Undisturbed
Uninvolved
Detached
Dispassionate

Perhaps it would help to look at who I was *not*. I was not...
Involved
Engaged
Compassionate
Aware
Supportive
Uncomfortable
Disturbed
Present

Am I being too hard on myself? If you think so, it may be because you identify with me. You may have been where I was. And maybe you're still there to some degree. All that difficult stuff went on in your city, too, in your larger world, and you're just glad it's over. Glad the good guys won. But the descriptions are spot on. And if these words don't paint the picture well, Jesus used some rather pejorative illustrations of those who lived in the proximity of need and did nothing, just like me. Where was I? At best, I was the priest or the Levite in Luke 10 who skirted a messy crime scene and traveled on the other side of the road. At worst, I was in the company of the goats described in Matthew 25 who looked on Jesus when he suffered poverty and hunger and thirst and offered no relief. Where was I? I was absent.

But what about now? You may protest, "I wasn't even born in the '60s. There is no legal discrimination now like there was with Jim Crow. Hasn't affirmative action worked? Our president is African American, after all. People of color are in positions of leadership and privilege in Memphis." Yes, these things are true. But take a deeper look into every urban area of our country. Poverty among people of color is still at tragic proportions. Inner-city schools are failing all over the country. Prisons overflow with people of color in astounding numbers, largely due to the "war on drugs," marking them for life as they carry the title "ex-felon." What's wrong now?

Rather than cast stones, the question I pose to myself and to those reading this book is, "Where am I?" and "What does God call me to do now?" Am I the priest, the Levite, or am I the Good Samaritan? Am I engaged or detached? Am I "fighting for justice" for the least, the lost, and left behind, or am I sitting on the sidelines? Oh, I might write a check, make a donation to agencies that "serve the poor." I might do a Thanksgiving basket for the less fortunate. But am I engaged? Am I a part of the solution? Am I on the side of justice, of the poor, the oppressed and the weary?

How Kind of Us to Flee

In 1973, five years after the sanitation workers' strike, the U.S. district court ordered Memphis schools to desegregate. Where was the white, "born again," conservative, Bible-believing, evangelical church then? Some of them were hastily forming a committee: Citizens Against Busing (CAB). That year CAB founded twenty-six schools and enrolled more than 5,000 students in them. Oh, the reason given for the mass production of new schools was the need for "Christian education" in order to avoid secular humanism and teaching about evolution, but no one doubted the real reason: race.

The busing of Memphis students proceeded without violence and the CAB claimed that their formation of so many new institutions helped to prevent it! (By the way: just one year after the court order, fewer than six of those schools, with 500 students enrolled, remained in existence.)[11]

Beyond Racism

This book is not just about racism. It is not even about *my* racism. It is about something central to every believer in Christ in every generation and in every setting. In my journey of repentance from the sin of racism, I have learned to go beyond the "Am I really a racist?" question to probe even deeper.

In his classic work *Christ and Culture*, Richard Niebuhr asks: Are we following the Christ of scripture or the Christ of

---

11 Joseph Watras, *Politics, Race, and Schools: Racial Integration, 1954-1994* (New York: Routledge, 2013), 57.

our particular culture? This is the question within the "Am I a racist?" question. In the South, the South I grew up in, the white evangelical church blindly followed the white, privileged, racist culture. In fact, embraced it. We lost sight of the Christ of scripture and, in our myopia, we stumbled headlong after an idea and a practice that reduced an entire race of our human family—our brothers and sisters "for whom Christ died" (1 Corinthians 8:11, NIV)—to something less than human.

Just as a child may grasp what she believes to be her father's hand and walk unsuspecting with a stranger until she looks up and discovers her mistake, Christians of my generation walked hand in hand with a "father" (the prevailing culture) who kept us safe and warm and prosperous. When we finally grasped that we had hold of the wrong hand is debatable. That it took us years to look up and discover our mistake is clear. That metaphor is telling, but it casts us as innocent children, and it turns the dismal act of mixing Christianity with racism into an accident rather than a sin. That's simply not accurate. And we're still reeling from these mistakes, trying to make things right. It's messy and the problems created by years of hatred and neglect continue to plague us. We wish they would just go away, these intractable issues of poverty, bigotry, hatred, paternalism, inadequate health care, failing urban school systems, a criminal justice system that is utterly broken. None of these "problems" happened overnight. They were years in the making and they will take years to overcome. It doesn't matter if you are eighty years old or eighteen, the sins of our past continue to ripple into our future. And we must continue to make things right.

Let's try another metaphor:

You know how a married couple can, over many years of intermingled life, begin to seem almost identical, even to the point that they begin to be considered a unit rather than separate? Like "Maw Maw and Paw Paw"? It's sweet evidence of the proximity and intimacy of two people. The scripture instructs us to pursue this same kind of metamorphosis in our relationship with Jesus. The result is a thing of beauty: "And we, who with unveiled faces all reflect the Lord's glory, are being transformed into his likeness with ever-increasing glory, which comes from the Lord, who is the Spirit." (2 Corinthians 3:19, NIV)

We are to be a mirror that reflects Jesus in our world. As we know all too well, everything around us threatens to draw our attention away from him and his Word, thus dimming and distorting the reflection. Paul warned the Romans of the very tendency Niebuhr wrote about in *Christ and Culture*:

Don't become so well-adjusted to your culture that you fit into it without even thinking. Instead, fix your attention on God. You'll be changed from the inside out. Readily recognize what he wants from you, and quickly respond to it. Unlike the culture around you, always dragging you down to its level of immaturity, God brings the best out of you, develops well-formed maturity in you. (Romans 12:2, MSG)

There you have it. How else could Christians in Western culture justify slavery and racism? Instead of molding our lives according to Christ's image, we spent three centuries molding Christ into our own image. We still do, don't we?

Sure, we can be countercultural at times, when a particular issue grips us. When I was in my twenties, an evangelical icon spoke before the Memphis City Council about the horrors of the sex industry. There was a huge campaign to get as many "born again" Christians as possible out to that meeting to support the fight against the strip clubs in town. Morally, this high-profile leader fixated on an evil that is indeed reprehensible, but I don't recall any evangelical leaders rising to the occasion when the sanitation workers pled with our city to treat them like men ten years earlier. As an institution, the evangelical church has proved over and over that she does indeed know how to take action, particularly in areas that she deems a measurable moral transgression like abortion, strip clubs or same-sex marriage. But where race or justice have been concerned, we have adopted all the wrong actions. In fact, racism wasn't defined as a sin at all. For reasons we'll discuss later on, the church has historically found it easier to remain distinct from the culture, even challenging it, on a narrowly defined moral front than to fight the tides of injustice on behalf of others. It's as if we try on the sayings of Jesus for size, pick and choose what fits, and discard the rest.

By the time my generation came along, Evangelicalism and culture were entangled intimately in this downward spiral, so that not only did the church mimic culture, but the culture mimicked the church. It's hard to say who co-opted whom. Like the married couple who resemble each other, it was difficult to tell which of our values were rooted in culture and which were rooted in scripture. Some express a longing for those days—when the general morals and mores of society supported what conservative Christians taught their children—as if those were our "well-adjusted" days. But, in far too many ways, we followed the downward tug. We adopted an uncanny ability to ignore the poor. We overlooked injustice. We justified disinheriting an entire people group from the human race.

In Paul's words, we find it too easy to become "well-adjusted" to a culture that drags us "down to its level." The Christians in Rome faced this battle to stay maladjusted where the culture was concerned. Every church in every generation faces it. The church faces it today. I face it every day. That's why it's so important to figure out where we were then and where we are now, to triangulate our position with a clear view of the culture and of Christ. We need a reference point, and the friend of sinners and tax collectors is where we must begin, the Jesus Christ of scripture.

Where was the church in Memphis in 1968? Where we just might end up again if we're not careful.

Whatcha gonna do?

1. Write out your own definition of racism. If applicable, you may want to try several versions of this, composing definitions for different time periods in your own personal history.
2. How connected do you feel to the racism of the civil rights movement era? Was it part of your experience? Do you feel in any way responsible for it? Were you in any way a victim of it?
3. Do you see racist attitudes today? Where? How are they displayed?
4. Whatever your age, how do you or have you experienced the "sins of our fathers/mothers" as it relates to racial polarization today?
5. What are the present issues in your city around race, poverty, and injustice, and how has the past impacted these issues?

Chapter 3

Relationships

In Living Color

History will have to record that the greatest tragedy of this period of social transition was not the strident clamor of the bad people, but the appalling silence of the good people.

—Martin Luther King Jr.

Greater love has no one than this, that someone lay down his life for his friends. You are my friends if you do what I command you.

—John 15:13-14, ESV

Truth is on the side of the oppressed.

—Malcolm X

In 1993, long after the specter of racism had haunted me enough to make me do something about it, I sat with a group of my peers in a pastors' advisory board meeting at an African American church located on the northern boundary of Orange Mound. Orange Mound is the African American neighborhood my wife and two girls had "relocated" to in 1977. For me, Orange Mound was the geographical vortex of a new approach to ministry, a new way to live life, in many

21

ways a new theology. But in 1993, all that was a decade and a half behind me.

In 1993, we were enlightened. Progressive. Black and white pastors, an equal number of each, met together to plan a citywide experiment in racial healing. We would directly confront racism and empower churches to become agents of reconciliation. Memphis Leadership Foundation, which I founded in 1987, had been up and running for some years, and we were able to "loan" Howard Eddings, our vice president, to the LifeFocus movement, providing executive leadership. That year, over 120 churches got involved in small groups to meet around the issue of racial reconciliation. The idea centered around Jesus's priestly prayer as recorded by John in the 17th chapter of his gospel. Jesus prayed for believers to be one as He and the Father are one, and further, that this oneness in Christ would be a testimony to the world around us that Jesus is the Christ. We were attempting to come together as one in order to demonstrate to Memphis the reconciling power of the gospel, spiritually, racially, and socially, a bold attempt to be the Church of Memphis.

The pastors' meeting was cordial and inviting. Unlike the rallies of a bygone era, the air wasn't fraught with racial tension, fear, or the undercurrent of animosity, that is, until the host pastor spoke.

During breakfast, he broke the gentle mood of camaraderie when he said, "We don't need an event, we need relationships...Gentlemen [you read that right, no female pastors at the table yet!], next door to this church sits an exclusive country club, one of Memphis's oldest monuments to racism and white privilege. I can't join that club. I can't have dinner there because I'm black. Yet there are members in the white churches on this advisory committee who belong to that club."

You could have heard a pin drop.

"There's something horribly wrong when we can sit here in the shadow of that monument to racism and discuss racial reconciliation. What we need, Gentlemen, is to become friends with one another, authentic friends. If we do that, then you will see me differently and I will see you differently, because we are friends."

The pastor was right. Friendship was exactly what we needed. Friendship is the very thing that chipped away at my own racist views. It still is.

New Eyes

In the years following 1968, I began to ask questions: How could Dr. King follow the same Christ that those who hated him and discriminated against African Americans followed? Was the Jesus I grew up with really the Jesus of history or was he the Jesus invented by culture? Was the Jesus Martin Luther King worshipped the Jesus of scripture or someone invented to justify his actions? These questions took years to answer.

In the meantime, I was building relationships of my own. In junior high I began to make forays "across the tracks" into north Memphis to play basketball. It didn't occur to me then that some of the kids I hung out with for hours on the courts had fathers or uncles who were the "garbage men" whose cry for dignity and respect brought Martin Luther King to Memphis. Although the two separate school systems that had existed until then—one black and one white—had been legally disbanded, Memphis schools were still basically segregated. My junior and senior high schools were some of the few exceptions. Although there was a black minority in our junior and senior high schools, I vividly remember that the principal and many of the teachers and coaches displayed distinctly racist attitudes. The demographics were changing, but the feelings weren't.

I became co-captain of our high school basketball team as a senior and I enjoyed significant relationships with players who didn't look like me. Four African Americans played on the team. These friendships deepened my personal experience with the fissure between our races. Our basketball coach was old school and did little in the way of encouraging African Americans to try out for the team. Many fine athletes didn't even bother. Our games were often held in the afternoon, especially if a white school was playing a black school. Often when our team traveled to a white school, both the black and the white players caught the wrath of the opposing student body. We whites were called "nigger lovers." My black teammates fared far worse. At black schools they were called "Oreos" or "Uncle Toms." Suddenly, the pain of racism became real. It became something I could no longer ignore because it was happening to teammates. It got up close and personal.

Two of my peers in high school had parents who were deeply involved in the civil rights ovement. In fact, they were icons in our city, heroes in the African American communities and demons in the white. Through them I was introduced, not only to a new way of thinking, but also to a network of people I would never have met in my white milieu. These new relationships made it difficult to hide in the relative comfort my own white culture. I was forced to confront my own racism and my own feelings of white superiority and privilege. Because of relationships, I began to look at my world through different eyes.

Speeding Up the Process

For a chemical reaction to occur, molecules must collide. The faster the molecules collide, the faster the reaction. Chemists often use a catalyst—an added substance—to either speed up or inhibit a reaction. For example, if you are trying to determine what gas is released from hydrogen peroxide, you might spend weeks in the lab watching a test tube to get an answer. But if you introduce manganese dioxide into the experiment, you would—within minutes—discover that oxygen is the gas released. This kind of catalyst is known as a positive catalyst, or a promoter.[12]

Changing a deeply imbedded thought process, like racism, takes time. It takes time in the mind of one person. It takes more time for the mindset of a community to change. It may take years for old thought patterns to ebb and the "renewed mind" Paul prescribes in Romans 12 to emerge. But what if you introduced a "promoter" into the mix?

I am convinced I would still be watching the ideological test tube of my own racist thinking if not for the positive catalyst of relationships. Relationships took what would have remained a purely pedantic exercise and turned it into real life change. Come to think of it, any biblical, life-altering truth is downright anemic if pursued in a relational vacuum. Friendships cause the reaction to that truth. Relationships instigate the real revolution.

Who is Jesus?

New relationships prompted new thinking. During this time I was introduced to the writings of Martin Luther King Jr., Malcolm X, W.E. Dubois, Richard Wright, and others. The scathing critique of Christianity in the autobiography of Malcolm X arrested me. I was beginning to believe he was right. My culture—and I—had fashioned Christ into a white, middle-class and American image. In my mind, Jesus was just like me. He was comfortable. He didn't demand all that much. Just go to church and don't sin too much, and you're

---

12 http://www.purchon.com/chemistry/catalyst.htm

okay. As long as I could say with some level of conviction that "Jesus is my personal Lord and Savior" or that I had "accepted Jesus" into my life, I was fine.

The only evils I was warned against in church were alcohol, drugs, cigarettes, vulgar language, and sex. Never injustice, abuse of privilege, oppression, or racism. My older brother went off to a Christian college and was required to sign an agreement that he wouldn't smoke, drink, play cards, or go to movies. That was the definition of discipleship: keep your nose clean morally. Loving your neighbor, pursuing social justice, meeting the needs of the poor, feeding the hungry... these standards didn't even merit a mention in the script. I saw two divergent options: I could become a liberal activist or a conservative moralist and the latter didn't make much sense, really.

I wanted to follow Jesus, but which one? The Jesus of white Evangelicalism who perched on the far right and accused the liberal church and black activists—the ones who supported the civil rights movement—of not being really saved? Or the "new" Jesus that I was reading and hearing about. As I approached my eighteenth birthday, I began to wonder if the "liberals" and the African American Christians got it right and the Evangelicals believed a gospel that was irrelevant at best and unbiblical at worst. Talk about a crisis of belief!

During high school I was involved in a ministry called Young Life, an international youth outreach ministry that targets teenagers on their turf with the truth claims of the gospel. A wise young woman who was a Young Life staffer at the time sensed my struggle and gave me some good advice: she told me to read the gospels. She suggested I read them with my mind as open as possible, as if I'd never read them before, never heard of Jesus. At the same time, the father of one of my peers who was one of those civil rights icons suggested I try reading them as if I were black, as if I was being discriminated against. It took some mental gymnastics, but I did it. And I discovered a Jesus who was altogether different from the invention of my culture. In fact, this Jesus sat in judgment of my culture. This Jesus was the most loving and the most radical person I had ever met. He was the friend of sinners, of the poor, the leper, the prostitute, the tax gatherer. *This* was a friend I wanted to know better.

If you were to read through the Bible in one year using two highlighter colors—marking words like rich or wealth with one color and words like poor, widows, orphans, oppressed with another color—you might be surprised at what you find. Contrary to teaching about prosperity today, an overwhelming majority of the passages dealing with wealth are negative. If you want to know who gets God's preferential treatment, it is the poor, the marginalized, and the oppressed. You might even conclude that God is biased on behalf of the least, the lost, the left out, and the left behind! I did.

If the gospel is the good news that God, in Christ, longs to call us *friends*, then, to be truly like him, our choice of friends should look a lot like his. This has been the pivotal point in my own repentance from racism. Yes, I have learned to say I value the "least of these" in my community, but it is relationships that have made what I claim to be true, actually true.

Withness and Whiteness

I went off to college and immediately entered the same tension that plagued me in my upbringing. I tutored and coached inner-city kids in Memphis *and* I was a volunteer leader at a Young Life club in one of Memphis's most exclusive suburbs. My time was spent yo-yoing between two very different neighborhoods.

Young Life taught me the rudiments of incarnational ministry. We didn't invite kids to a church building; we went to them where they lived. We met kids on their own turf: the basketball courts, the football games, the hangout places. We "earned the right to be heard" as we developed friendships. It was a ministry of being present.

Young Life holds "club" meetings in the homes of kids involved, but the program isn't the real genius of the ministry: "withness" is. While I was learning this ministry of "withness" through Young Life, my involvement in inner-city neighborhoods in Memphis helped loosen the noose of "whiteness" and middle-class culture that was still around my neck. Perhaps I began tutoring and coaching as a vague attempt to atone for my whiteness and privilege, but I quickly fell in love with the kids, the work, and the community. Again, relationships trumped everything. These two experiences, one that taught me the basics of incarnational theology and mission and the other that taught me about God's heart for the poor and my own white privilege, would shape the rest of my life.

The summer after my freshman year in college I served for six weeks on the summer staff at one of Young Life's camps in Colorado, Frontier Ranch, high in the Rockies. Each week, several hundred high school kids from Young Life areas across the country come to Frontier to have a great time and to hear the gospel expertly communicated in their own language and imagery. In the first two weeks, the buses unloaded all white kids. The next four weeks were dubbed "urban camps," with kids coming from New York City's Lower East Side, Chicago's West Side, and New York's Chinatown, among others. A new staff was brought in, including Dean Borgman, who is currently a professor at Gordon-Conwell Theological Seminary. He worked with "urban kids" in New York City. Back then, "urban" was code language for black, Asian, and Latino kids living in the "ghetto." Dean was a scrawny white guy whose rapport with kids made an indelible impression on me.

I was a biology major and had wanted to be a doctor for

as long as I could remember, but ministry began to steal my heart that summer in the Rockies. By the time I was a junior in college, I sensed that God was calling me, not only into ministry, but into the same kind of neighborhoods Dean Borgman worked in. I was hooked.

I approached the area director of Young Life in Memphis and told him I wanted to start Young Life in the inner city of Memphis after I graduated from college. At that time, Young Life was a robust ministry in Memphis. Though a few of the "clubs" were somewhat integrated, the ministry targeted predominantly white kids in suburban-type schools. There were volunteer leaders at one high school who proactively reached both the white and the black students, but that eventually led to the formation of two clubs in the same school. The area director was enthusiastic about starting "urban Young Life" in the urban core of Memphis, but he was one of just a handful who caught the vision.

While waiting for a staff position to open up, I taught science and coached basketball at a predominantly African American high school. Then, in the fall of 1975, I was officially accepted on staff with the charge to begin Young Life in an inner-city neighborhood.

I began to do what all Young Life staffers do: build relationships with kids on their turf. The main difference between my years as a Young Life volunteer in the suburbs and now wasn't the methodology, it was the geography, the turf.

I did everything I'd been taught to do in order to get to know kids at Melrose High School in Orange Mound, one of the country's oldest and largest African American neighborhoods west of Harlem, but the school was African American and I was white. The racial tension at that time was still high. The kids didn't know what to make of me. I was there all the time, but it was slowgoing. Some people thought I was an undercover cop. Others thought I was a drug dealer, or worse.

Finally, after months of what is known in Young Life par-
lance as "contact work" or "winning the right to be heard," I
held our first club meeting. I handed out fliers the week before
and invited every kid I knew on campus. Three guys showed
up. And one of them lived in the house where we held the
club! Undaunted, we continued to have club every week for
the rest of the school year. Attendance never exceeded ten.
Compared with the suburban club I'd led as a volunteer that
averaged close to 100 every week, this was a depressing start.
Another one of Young Life's approaches is summer camping.
I got four guys to attend a camp in North Carolina in the
summer of 1976. Today, one is a pastor, another is a surgeon,
and one is an accountant.

By most measures, you could call that first year of Young
Life Urban in Memphis a failure. But I was learning something that would shape the years ahead: friendships are
essential and they don't form overnight.

Grace

*The more friendships I made and the more I read the words
of black writers, the deeper my embarrassment at the color
of my skin became. A nagging sense that I owed some sort
of penance drove many of my early activities. And still, the
guilt over who I was and what I represented lingered.*

*Why would a black man in Memphis in the 1970s want
to befriend me? Especially if that friendship was proffered by
a man he suspected of caring more about his own redemption than the relationship? The only answer is grace. I didn't
deserve anything but mistrust and hatred for what my race
had inflicted upon theirs, but still my new friends accepted
me. I was awkward and my motives weren't always pure, but
they loved me anyway. Thus, my first lessons in city ministry were lessons in grace.*

"There's Something Horribly Wrong"

Today, when people visit our ministry, they often comment about the number of African Americans in Memphis. They visit from cities like Indianapolis or Tulsa, and they just aren't prepared for a city that looks a whole lot more colorful than theirs. It doesn't just look that way, it *is* that way. Our population is approximately 61 percent black, 34 percent white, 4 percent other, or mixed, and 1 percent Asian.[13]

These are some of the same people who, when nudged about racism, shrug their shoulders and say things like, "I wasn't even born when the civil rights movement was going on," or "*I* didn't own a slave," or "*I* don't see color." These are typically Caucasians who live in suburbs or exurbs where race is not an up-front, presenting issue. Sure, their social setting or their workplace is less homogeneous than a generation ago. Their worldview is different and fresh. Ask them about racism, and it is clear they assume it's over and done with, old news. They are proud to announce that they're colorblind. But then they visit us in Memphis or they penetrate inner-city pockets of their own cities, and racism and systemic discrimination become palpably real. The old lines still drawn in the sand, the institutional racism of our past and present, the lack of communication and respect; it's all still there. The erosion process isn't over yet.

I'm not sure the central underlying question is, "Why are there so many African Americans in one city?" I wonder, instead, if we shouldn't ask, "Where did all the white people go?" Students in the former Memphis City Schools (there was a merger between the city and county school system in 2013) are over 86 percent black, not quite 8 percent white, 4 percent Hispanic, and 1 percent Asian.[14] These statistics ought to pro-

---

13 http://www.idcide.com/citydata/tn/memphis.htm

14 http://www.localschooldirectory.com/district-schools/791/Memphis-City-School-District/TN

voke the more unsettling question. Maybe over 75 percent of the white households in Memphis do not have school-age children in them, but that's not likely. It is far more probable that those children are in the private schools or suburban county schools. Think "white flight" is a thing of the past? Think again. And, these days, it isn't just the white people who are leaving the city and its schools. The middle and upper middle class—regardless of race—are jumping ship as well. And while there is a move to re-gentrify central city areas in most major cities, often at the expense of the poor who are displaced, there are pockets of poverty in the urban core that seem too desperate to ever be transformed back to the once vibrant neighborhoods of the past. And with the three plus decades of "white flight," and in many instances, "middle-class flight" from the public school system, we are witnessing a dismal educational reality for the future of our city and other cities like it. The economic reality of an undereducated workforce is a major issue facing America. A program here in Memphis called the Memphis Teacher Residency Program often declares that the public education debacle in America is today's biggest civil rights or justice issue.

But it looks like we're doing better, doesn't it? Take another look at Memphis today. Rather, take a look at the evangelical church in the South. Our vocal, public recompense for our past racism is commendable. Churches and even denominations have "confessed" their racism of the past. Some sanctuaries are trying, at least, to reflect the diversity they advertise on billboards. Our raw honesty, when confronted with past sins, is admirable. Or is it?

These steps may be well-intentioned. But, in an eerie sense, our actions seem once again in perfect step with the culture. Just as the church has adapted to the world around us in other areas—architecturally, musically, technologically—we've done so in our social posture as well. Our cities decry racism and often blame the church for how entrenched she became in it. Our cities champion diversity. And so it *looks like* the church is keeping up. She's moving slowly, as usual, but we do eventually follow the trends, don't we?

But what does any of this have to do with relationships? Is it just slick marketing? Is it even *real*? If so, why do we still struggle with feelings of superiority or inferiority in our dealings with each other? Do we really get it? Who are our friends? How much like us are they? Okay, maybe their skin color is different. But what about these other markers: economic background, economic status, tastes, slang, theology, ecclesiology, accent, politics, and education? I'm not talking about projects or programs—I'm talking about deep, abiding relationships, the real deal. Have we done what Niebuhr suggested? Are we following a fad on the barest surface rather than following Christ in the deepest crevices of life? Could it be we are only giving lip service here? Could it be we're like the denizens of Oz, wearing the green eyeglasses everyone else has on and, therefore, just as blind to the way things really are?

Friendships are not formed behind the lecterns of large churches. Nor are they fashioned by making a supersized declaration on a sign. If we believe that, we're following yet another trend, the one that equates intention with action. Relationship is much grittier, messier, more real-life than that. While relationships comprised the crucible in which the major changes in my own life have taken and still take place, I don't want to display my own experience as the standard here. After all, I have yet to literally lay my life on the line for my friends. I want to be that kind of friend, but I'm not yet.

Again, it is all too easy to allow the culture to define things for us. What is friendship? Ask culture that question and it's easy to figure out. Just watch your television, read some pop-psychology books, poll the neighborhood. Friendship is all about win-win, "me" time, and finding ways we are alike. It's sentimental. Its heft about as light as a greeting card.

But how does Jesus define friendship? If we look at what eyewitnesses observed about him, friendship is a shocking, preferential relationship with sinners, outcasts, and "the least" of society (Matthew 11:19, Luke 7:34, ESV). It is startling to note that Jesus even called Judas his friend. He embraced his betrayer as a friend when the man was in the very act of betraying him! (Matthew 26:50, ESV) In John 15, we get the most complete description of friendship in the New Testament. Jesus tells his followers that he is not only their Master, he is also their friend. He says, "I have called you friends." This kind of friendship is…

• Demonstrated by a love that is willing to die (verse 13)
• Characterized by intimate knowledge (verse 15)
• Is proactive (verse 16)…Jesus chose them

The flavor of the Incarnation is friendship: "The Word became flesh and blood, and moved into the neighborhood." (John 1:14, MSG) If this is who Jesus is, and if we are called to be like him, to live his life in the world, then incarnation means intimacy. And intimacy is best fostered in proximity. We need to be the kind of friend Jesus was. *Close*, in every sense of the word.

That is precisely why racism still needs to be addressed today. Because it is a wedge between friends. If I hold on to any shred of racism in my attitudes and feelings toward you, then you are not valuable enough to me for me to lay down my life for you. Racism gives me the upper hand of superiority, rather than the outstretched hand of love and humility. It makes friendship, by any definition—especially the ultimate definition given by Jesus—impossible. It creates distance. It divides. That's what it did in 1968, in 1993, and still does today. If we can't leave racism behind in the wake of true friendship, then the pastor who pointed out the country club next door to his church that excluded people in his congregation was right, and something is horribly wrong.

Whatcha gonna do?

1. Take a moment to consider: What qualifies you to be Christ's friend? In what way are you the right "fit" or "flavor" so that his choice of you makes sense?
2. Take an inventory of your attachments—the relationships in which you freely give both "affection and esteem." What led you to choose those friends?
3. If you were to follow Christ in this area of your life, what would you change about your relationships, how you choose them, how you pursue them?
4. How might following Jesus's definition of friendship chip away at racism in your neighborhood and in your city?

Chapter 4
Relocation
A Ministry of Place

While the spirit of neighborliness was important on the frontier because neighbors were so few, it is even more important now because our neighbors are so many.

—Lady Bird Johnson

"Independence"... [is] middle-class blasphemy. We are all dependent on one another, every soul of us on earth.

—G.B. Shaw, *Pygmalion*, 1912

Tomorrow morning before we depart, I intend to land and see what can be found in the neighborhood.

—Christopher Columbus

The Word became flesh and blood, and moved into the neighborhood.

—John 1:14 MSG

A brochure showed up in our mailbox the other day. Beneath the words "Finding the Right Neighborhood" were four glossy photos of four stately homes on four perfectly manicured lawns. I was curious. The mailer urged potential home buyers to consider the primary influences on the home selection process: convenience to jobs, affordability, proximity to family and friends, and the quality of the school district. It then told the conscientious buyer to visit the libraries, restaurants, and retail centers nearby. Finally, the most meticulous were advised to spend time in the community at various times of day to get an accurate gauge of the noise and activity levels. "Are the homes well-maintained?" asks the brochure. "Is the environment peaceful?"

Now, I'm not knocking this approach. In fact, I think it sounds pretty smart. Wise, in fact. This is one of those areas where the party line of the culture makes perfect sense. Spend your hard-earned cash on the nicest, safest home you can buy. All that extra square footage and the pool?

In case you didn't know, church isn't the only place we're reminded to use our homes as centers for the common good. The entire backside of the flier, printed in a more subtle black and white, tells the new homeowner "how you can make your neighborhood a better place." A bullet-point list of ways to "make a difference" includes offering your professional expertise to neighbors because they just might reciprocate someday. Altruism is popular in just about every industry these days, including real estate. As long as you can still get the stuff you really want. As long as you can still live the dream.

I don't mean to sound cynical. And, if I do, it's because I struggle like everyone else with the upward pull of our consumer culture. It's just that we choose our homes a lot like we choose our friends: in sync with the culture instead of in sync with Jesus. *That's* the point I want to make here. As you hear the story about my family and the way we approached relocation, I don't want you to hear some self-flagellating, severe dictum. We didn't languish in our hovel wearing hair shirts. I don't advocate hardship simply for hardship's sake. I wouldn't call a single one of our relationships "difficult."

I also don't think being like Jesus and befriending the poor or those different from us means we don't enjoy friendships with those who do look like us. My wife Becky and I have a very wide circle of friends that we enjoy, and we are enriched by them all.

But I do want to challenge Christians to consider Christ instead of the culture in our decisions. If the original Incarnation was a literal relocation from heaven to earth, might we give some thought to a similar repositioning? I'm just asking. The metric here isn't "downward mobility"; it is much deeper than that. Just as Paul learned to function in want and in plenty, Becky and I have chosen our homes differently in every stage of our life together. This chapter highlights one of those stages. The central point isn't so much *where* we moved as it is *to whom* we looked for direction when we moved. Do we look to Christ or to culture?

From Outside to In

In the fall of 1976, after the summer camping experience, our Young Life clubs began to take off. We were averaging forty to fifty kids each week. Few of the homes in the neighborhood could accommodate such a crowd, so I rented a building and bought a ping-pong table. That worked for a while.

After college I married my high school sweetheart, Becky Blair, and we had the first of our four daughters. Our comfortable starter home was the perfect place for us. We had gotten a great deal on the house. It was in a white, stable neighborhood where the prices were appreciating nicely. We had a big backyard, a dog, and two cars. The house was one block from the church we attended with many of our good friends. It was minutes away from the best babysitters on the planet, Becky's parents and mine. Ministry was going well *and* we were living the American dream. Life was good.

But I was restless. I had what seemed to Becky like a 24/7 schedule of ministry in the neighborhood. I'm afraid that's an accurate assessment. The "center" wasn't meeting all of our needs. On some nights kids would show up and then leave because it was too crowded. We were paying rent for a place that was not quite fitting the bill. One night during "club," there was a shoot-out at a lounge a few doors down from the center. Not a great place for a bunch of teenagers. I was still, on many levels, an outsider in the community. In my impatience for change, I began to mentally poke holes in our American dream. I began to think about moving our family to the neighborhood where our entire ministry took place.

By this time I was acquainted with John Perkins, founder of Mendenhall Ministries and Voice of Calvary in Mississippi. These ministries were the forerunners of the Christian Community Development Association. CCDA is now the largest network for urban ministry in the world. Dr. Perkins later became a friend and mentor. As I read his books, I was intrigued by his assertion that ministry to the poor required relocation. Perkins asserted that relocation is incarnational ministry at its best. As long as you are an outsider, you never fully understand the dynamics of the community. You are forever what your geography claims you to be: outsider.

I was convinced we needed to move. Becky was not. She could only picture the potential dangers, not just the physical ones, but the emotional ones as well. Because of my busy schedule, she feared her isolation would only be exacerbated if we lived farther away from friends and family. She was perfectly content where we were; why change that? And the ministry was going great.

I went to two of my mentors, Fred Davis and Verley Sangster, with my enthusiastic plan. Each of them asked the same question: "Is Becky supportive of the idea and ready to do it?" I replied that she was not. Each man suggested that God may not be in this plan, at least not at this time. "If God is behind this, He will move in Becky's heart just like He is in yours. Just keep doing ministry and don't mention the move again," said Verley. Fred gave the same advice. And that's exactly what I did. (I'll tell more about these wise men—Fred in Memphis and Verley in Chicago—in chapter 6, but these conversations alone are proof of their value as friends and mentors.)

As we were nearing the end of our second year of Young Life ministry, Becky came home one afternoon in the spring of 1977 and handed me a real estate flier. On it was a picture of a house just down the street from the high school in Orange Mound.

"I've been driving around Orange Mound looking for homes and I found this. I think we should buy it."

Verley and Fred were right. Until that moment, I'm not sure I believed them. If I had disregarded their advice and pushed Becky, ours would not have been the first marriage to founder on the rocks of a "calling" perceived by only one of two spouses. I am convinced Becky would have gone along with the move eight months earlier had I forced the issue. She is that committed to our marriage and to the ministry. But I'm equally convinced that our marriage would have suffered. Ministry—engendered and led by the Holy Spirit— does not destroy marriages. Ministry—when we are called into it by God—does not create confusion. But stubbornness sure can.

Becky was my partner in ministry. She not only worked with me in club, she attended sporting events, started a Bible study (Young Life calls them campaigner groups) for the girls, and was deeply committed to our urban context. Every Sunday night, Becky made a huge meal and I'd pick up kids and bring them to our home for a time of exploring the Bible together. She already embraced the concept of incarnational ministry, so it just made sense that she would eventually embrace relocation as well.

The Orange Mound house was perfect. Huge backyard, patio, and garage. A big living room and den combination that could accommodate maybe seventy-five kids for club meetings. Two bedrooms, a bath and a half, and a study off of the living room for my office. We bought it, sold our other house, and moved in the fall of 1977. We were excited, but our families weren't. In fact, we didn't get a lot of support from them. They were afraid for us. Becky's father warned her that she and our daughters would surely be attacked and raped in our new neighborhood. There was a lot of fear in those days. The truth is, people in our new community had, historically, much more reason to fear *us* than we did to fear them.

Our ministry took off like never before. I was no longer an outsider. I was a member of the community. Kids were at our house all the time. We had our second daughter while living there and we had a constant supply of babysitters. Relocation is not for everyone. There are plenty of people who do effective urban ministry without relocating, but, for us, it was crucial.

Can We Save a City Like Sodom?

In his book A Theology as Big as the City, *Ray Bakke wonders about cities like Sodom, huge cities with huge problems. Are they salvageable? He asks: "Can a handful of people save a city? Can a few leaven the multitudes?"*

Bakke answers his own question with a resounding yes: "My stories could go on. Believe me when I say that ten Holy-Spirit-led men or women can pressure and even transform huge cities. It's happening everywhere. There is a

relationship always between the presence of the godly and the
preservation of urban communities."[15]
        This gives me hope for all cities. And it gives me hope for
mine in particular. Memphis is the place to which I am called.
That calling has unfolded in the chapters of my life over time,
with each chapter pointing me to Memphis. That's my story.
Your story, like you and like your city, will be unique. I have
to agree with Bakke: a little leaven can go a long way even in
the cities with the largest needs.

Jesus is the Ultimate Relocator...
But there are Others

A lot has been written lately about the city. I'm certainly not
the only one who cares about it. The city is so important that
it figures in our final, eternal destination. Biblical writers
describe heaven as a golden city with a garden planted smack
in the middle of its downtown. That sounds really hopeful;
yet, the odds are that the city you live in now doesn't have
a Garden of Eden downtown like our final urban home will
encircle. That's because, ever since Adam and Eve's eviction
from the first Eden, our world—and our cities—have been
broken. It's a chronic problem, a lot like poverty, homeless-
ness, urban decay. It is so systemic it seems eternally hope-
less. Sometimes it's so bad our human tendency is to run
away. But, throughout history, there have been those who
have run the other way; those who so ache for the dying city
that they run back into it. Like a firefighter charging back
into a burning building, they calculate the danger, don the
equipment, call for help, and go.

        In the scripture, Jerusalem plays the starring role as far as
cities are concerned. It is the quintessential city. I don't want

15 Ray Bakke, *A Theology As Big As the City* (Downers Grove: Intervarsity
    Press, 1997), 39.

to hijack Jerusalem for my own purposes here, but there are some parallels worth noting. "Salem"—Jerusalem's original name, one as old as Methuselah—means peace. It's basically the same ancient word as "shalom," a one-word description of God's original plan and ultimate desire for the city: peace. Clearly, God isn't finished with the city. His plan is to redeem it. To buy it back for his glory. To give it peace. I believe we can see glimpses of this heart of God today, just as the prophets and major players of scripture saw it then. Just as Jesus demonstrated it by relocating from heaven to the hills of Bethlehem and, ultimately, to the city of Jerusalem where he redeemed mankind for all time, crucified on a garbage heap.

Jerusalem, like our cities today, languished more often than it thrived. In Old Testament times it suffered most during the exile of its people to Babylon. The Jews didn't flee Jerusalem because they wanted to; they were forcibly expelled. But multiple prophets, both before, during, and after the exile, make it clear that this diaspora of God's people was due to their sin. (Could it be said our abandonment of our cities, in many cases, has the same root?)

Nehemiah was an expatriate of Jerusalem who lived in relative ease in another city, Susa, in ancient Babylon. His home was safe, civilized, fortified. He had a steady, somewhat prestigious job, if not at times dangerous! He was content. Or was he?

And then his brother brought him news from Jerusalem. He brought back news that shook Nehemiah to the core. The walls were broken down and the gates had been destroyed by fire. His city was in big trouble. There was no shalom in Jerusalem.

Nehemiah could have sighed and said, "That's really terrible. Things certainly are bad back home."

And that would have been that. But Nehemiah had a different response. Before the events began to unfold in his life that led him back to his city as a leader and a change agent, Nehemiah's *heart* relocated first. Everything within him changed. Take a look at the complete revamping of Nehemiah's heart in the first chapter of his book:

- He sat down—an immediate response.
- He wept—an emotional response.
- He mourned—a soulful response.
- He confessed—a moral response.
- He fasted—a desperate response.
- He prayed—a dependent response.

Nehemiah's initial response to the "trouble and shame" of his city provoked a chain reaction that changed history. An incarnational heart prompted incarnational action. I'm intrigued by the first thing Nehemiah did when he heard about the state of Jerusalem: "He sat down." I have observed this reaction many times. When people begin to be educated, up close, about the real needs of the city, they are paralyzed. The paralysis may only last for a moment, or a few days, or a season. But that's how bad things often are. The poverty, hunger, trafficking of young children, the many cycles of despair that exist beneath the thriving, healthy exteriors of our cities can do that to you when you really see it and think about it. I understand. I also understand Nehemiah's tears and grief. But the trigger of the action lies, I think, in the fact that he not only examined the problem, he shared the guilt. Nehemiah attributed the fact that his people were scattered and his city devastated, not to their enemies, but to their own sin. He didn't pass the buck. The twelve action-packed chapters that follow began with one man's humble, pliable heart, confession, and repentance. Had he simply confessed his own culpability then, that would have been that. Confession followed by repentance—now that's a different story. He took action; he went in a different direction.

Romanticize Relocation? Don't Even Think About it

If you know anything about Nehemiah, you recognize the names of the antagonists in the story, Sanballat and Tobiah. Before one worker picked up one tool, these two detractors began to drone like sand gnats in their faces:

When Sanballat the Horonite, Tobiah the Ammonite official, and Geshem the Arab heard about it, they laughed at us, mocking, "Ha! What do you think you're doing? Do you think you can cross the king?" I shot back, "The God-of-Heaven will make sure we succeed. We're his servants and we're going to work, rebuilding. You can keep your nose out of it. You get no say in this - Jerusalem's none of your business!" (Nehemiah 2:18-20, MSG)

Relocation is never without issues, and those issues usually present themselves on day one.

This is Our Neighborhood Now

By the time we moved to Orange Mound, institutional racism had had its way with our community for far too long. The things we took for granted just a few miles down the road were very different here. The police force, overwhelmingly white, operated more like an army of occupation than like sentries who were dedicated to serve and protect. Unemployment was high. The garbage wasn't collected in a timely manner like it was in the suburbs, suggesting a stinking déjà vu of 1968. There were maybe a handful of grocery stores or banks. Insurance premiums were higher. Securing a mortgage on a home was more difficult due to "redlining" of certain neighborhoods. A good portion of the homes in Orange Mound were owned by white, absentee landlords who allowed the homes in the neighborhood to deteriorate to slum conditions. A good friend of mine today lived in one of those homes. It was a shotgun duplex. A shotgun house is so narrow, usually one room wide, you can shoot a shotgun in the front door and hit everyone in the house. This friend and his family—two parents, several sisters and brothers—had little connection with the white world other than their landlord who came by to collect the rent.

One night during the Christmas season, while we were away from home, someone broke into our house. We returned home around nine o'clock and saw our neighbor from across the street sitting on our front porch. He had heard a crash inside our house and knew we weren't home, so he ran to investigate and frightened the would-be burglars away. The front door had been kicked in and he was protecting the house until we got home. He did not call the cops because he was fairly certain they would arrest him if he did. This was before the cell phone era, so he had no way of calling us. He kept his vigil in the cold until we returned. We called to file a police report for insurance purposes and, true to form, the police showed up well over an hour later. After they checked our home for intruders, they left, shaking their heads and asking us rudely why on earth we lived there.

"This is *our* neighborhood," I protested. What happened here happened to *us*. We were no longer "those people." The men who, a decade before, had carried signs begging the world to acknowledge that they were men, real people with real homes, real lives, real needs, some of those men were now my neighbors. Until I began to know them as my friends who lived next door or down the street or one block over, I never really *saw* them. I was sheltered and protected. Ignorant.

Our ministry was in full swing: Young Life clubs, campaigners Bible studies, coaching baseball. We added tutoring to the mix and, once again, living among our neighbors enriched that experience as well. We were the ones who got an education. One day a young man showed up at our house for tutoring and I asked him where his textbook was. He explained that the teacher would not let the students bring books home. There were not enough to go around. Later I found out that in the days of segregation, the black schools obtained used books from the white school system when those schools bought new ones. Same thing with athletic equipment and uniforms: the black schools got the hand-me-downs. Just as the sanitation workers' conditions were an unknown piece in my "Don't Ask, Don't Tell" education about racism, I had no idea.

Like the mounds of refuse that littered Memphis streets and backyards in 1968, the issues in our new neighborhood ten years later began to heap like a heavy load in my heart. Adults and kids faced tremendous barriers to employment. Many young men who had been incarcerated, often on minor offenses, found it virtually impossible to get work. Some children went to school without breakfast and struggled to learn while hunger gnawed at them; a child couldn't see the chalkboard but had never been to an optometrist; and another teenager landed time after time in juvenile court when he believed the only way to survive being teased because he couldn't read was to fight.

To relocate is to bear burdens. And those burdens are far too cumbersome to carry alone. This story would end right here if Becky and I had relocated in one big, noble solitary attempt to save Orange Mound. But we didn't, and it doesn't end here. It goes on. In the next chapter you'll meet some of the people who complete the story. Relocation is not about saving anything or anyone; it's about being a neighbor. Relocation is one of the 'three R's' of Christian community development as described by John Perkins and his disciples in the Christian Community Development Association. The other two R's are reconciliation and redistribution.[16] Relocation is often misunderstood, particularly when relocation is done with a superior attitude, or with an attitude that somehow moving in will make things better. No, it's about being a neighbor; it's about identifying with the community. It's about becoming an insider rather than an outsider. Yes, the "relocater" may bring some skills or talents to the community, adding to the assets already there. I see it more as a demonstration of presence, a demonstration of the Incarnation. The second "R" is for reconciliation and by this we mean racial, cultural, and class reconciliation. It means bringing people and communities together across racial, cultural, ethnic, and class divides. Obviously, reconciliation is at the heart of the gospel. Paul states it this way in II Corinthians 5:18ff: "All this is from God, who *reconciled* us to himself through Christ and gave us the ministry of reconciliation: that God was reconciling the world to himself in Christ not counting people's sins against them and he has committed to us the message of reconciliation..." Reconciliation, then, is central to community development, just as is relocation which, of course, mirrors the Incarnation. The last R of Christian community development is redistribution. What is meant by this is not taking from the rich and giving to the poor. I've heard Dr. Perkins say time and again that "if you took money from the rich and gave to the poor, the rich would have the money back tomorrow!" No, it's not that. Rather, redistribution happens when those inside and outside a community recognize the assets that are there and begin to build on those, thus "redistributing" opportunities for new investment. It's about increasing opportunities for community growth and development, like creating business opportunities, thus providing job opportunities. It's about getting great teachers in failing schools like the Memphis

---

16 John M. Perkins, *Let Justice Roll Down: A Strategy for Community Development* (Ventura, CA: Regal Books, 2011), 54-55.

Teacher Residency program is doing (you can find out more about MTR by going to their website memphistr.org), thus "redistributing talent. Or it could be by building new homes or senior citizen housing that's safe and affordable, thus redistributing tax dollars and improving property values. The three R's of relocation, reconciliation, and redistribution are all tied together when it comes to ministry in the urban context. It's a holistic gospel we live and preach.

Whatcha gonna do?

1. How educated are you—really—about your city? What can you do to learn more?
2. Look at the progression Nehemiah went through when he first heard about Jerusalem. Have you experienced any of these reactions to the state of your city? How so, and when?
   a. He sat down
   b. He wept
   c. He mourned
   d. He confessed
   e. He fasted
   f. He prayed
3. In chapter 2, Nehemiah petitions the king for permission to relocate. Is relocating an option for you? If not, are the barriers surmountable?
4. Is your family on board with the direction of your ministry? Have you had that discussion lately?

Chapter 5
The Gospel
Spiritual or Social?

Whenever Jesus healed, he rendered a social service to his fellows.[17]

—Walter Rauschenbusch, in *The Social Principles of Jesus*

Maycomb gave them Christmas baskets, welfare money, and the back of his hand.[18]

—Harper Lee, in *To Kill A Mockingbird*

And the Word became flesh, and dwelt among us, and we beheld His glory, glory as of the only begotten from the Father, full of grace and truth.

—John 1:14 (ESV)

We all know what it's like to experience that moment when a pendulum reaches the farthest reach of its arc and begins the dramatic swing back to its opposite pole. It happens all the time. We overeat from Thanksgiving to Christmas, until

---

17   Walter Rauschenbusch, *The Social Principles of Jesus* (Toronto: University of Toronto Libraries, 1920), 4.

18   Harper Lee, *To Kill a Mockingbird* (New York: Harper, 50th Anniversary Edition, 2010), 317.

New Year's Eve ushers in a drastic reversal in behavior called *diet and exercise* because, according to the scale, things have simply gone too far. A little seasonal excess suddenly threatens to become gluttony. Our kids end their summer vacations desperately needing the imposition of a schedule, because a little too much relaxation threatens to become laziness. This pattern occurs in society as well. Two generations ago, for example, the medical community advocated formula feeding for babies and discouraged mothers from breastfeeding... until women began to wonder whether the doctors were wrong. A movement called the La Leche League encouraged mothers to go back to their grandmothers' example, standing in opposition to revered medical wisdom, all because a little science threatened to take over good old common sense.

Revolutions are sparked at the farthest arc of a pendulum. When a social construct becomes so unbearably close to *wrong* that something has to happen. When we've waited long enough and action must be taken. From the Reformation to the Great Awakening to the "Jesus Movement" of the 1970s, the church has had its share of pendulum swings as well. It seems as if we're always either reaching one extreme or another, doesn't it? Or, in reaction to that extreme, we're heading straight toward its opposite.

Are we Greek or Hebrew?

If you simply observe this universal tendency to get off balance, it certainly appears that the Greeks were right: life is a two-sided wonder. It is inherently dualistic. And, in many ways, that's true. But the Greeks went so far as to say that there are two parallel but not intersecting realities, the physical and the spiritual. This worldview, called Gnosticism or Docetism, has heavily influenced Western thought since the first two centuries.

According to the Gnostics, the physical was evil and the spiritual was good. Therefore, Jesus could not have come in the flesh because flesh was evil. He only "appeared" to become a physical being. In his epistles, John the Apostle had strong words to say about this idea which had begun to raise its head in the early church, what we might call proto Gnosticism: "Every spirit that acknowledges that Jesus Christ has come in the flesh is from God, but every spirit that does not acknowledge Jesus is not from God." (I John 4:2-3, NIV) Or: "Many deceivers, who do not acknowledge Jesus Christ as coming in the flesh, have gone out into the world. Any such person is the deceiver and the antichrist." (II John 7, NIV) Obviously, I'm over-simplifying a complex issue, but the point is that the Gnostic worldview completely separated the physical realm from the spiritual. To achieve salvation, the goal for a believer was to "escape" the physical that held the spirit captive and ascend through a series of mystical steps by gaining knowledge (gnosis) of the truly spiritual.

As crazy as it sounds, the conservative Christian culture I grew up in embraced a version of this Gnosticism in our approach to life and ministry. Evangelism in those days focused on one goal alone: the salvation of souls. And after conversion, discipleship defined Christian maturity in terms of sin management. The more sinless you were, the more mature you were. Involvement in fair housing laws, civil rights, voters' rights, social justice, combating racism, or education reform had no place in Christian ministry. We were only to be involved with winning souls to Christ. In my early years as a Young Life volunteer I was taught that Christian discipleship included two vertical dimensions: prayer and Bible study, and two horizontal dimensions: witnessing and fellowship. You may remember the wheel illustration of the obedient Christian life with Christ at the center of these four spokes. The wheel had no spokes to represent social involvement, loving our neighbors, feeding the hungry, compassion or justice, themes that are equally illustrated in the Bible and throughout church history as crucial aspects of Christian discipleship. The Kingdom of God was all about the spiritual, and not one iota about the physical except as it related to personal morality.

How could we have gotten so far off base? you may be wondering. And I don't blame you. I think we can chalk it up to a pendulum swing, a reaction to an imbalance. Early in the 1900s, Walter Rauschenbusch wrote several books that made "the social gospel" a household term in many "liberal" churches. (In light of the rather gnostic worldview of my day, I found his works—which I read years later—quite helpful.) By the 1930s, those that adhered to the "social gospel," embraced the idea that Christian ministry was about reforming society and the "immense latent perfectibility in human nature." Having rejected the basic tenets of the gospel—including sin and forgiveness—this view was all about the physical and very little about the spiritual. No wonder conservative "Evangelicals and Fundamentalists" reacted. But by the time I was a young believer, intent on doing ministry "right," the conservative evangelical culture in which I found myself had certainly swung too far in the opposite direction, severing evangelism from any social justice issue.

The questions I began to ask were these: Is the gospel *merely* personal? Are its implications exclusively spiritual? As long as I say a short prayer and affirm that Jesus is my Personal Savior, am I saved and heaven bound? How do you reconcile this tract-sized edition of the good news with the social gospel? You can't, if you think like the ancient Greek Gnostic. You have to think like a Hebrew instead.

Jesus, according to his own words, is our Savior, but he is more than that, much more. In the Hebrew worldview, humanity is a whole: spiritual, emotional, cultural, mental, and physical. Jesus provides the perfect model for this world-view. He preached *and* he healed. He fed the masses truth *and* bread. Of all the people he delivered and healed and even raised from the dead, it wasn't always clear whether or not they followed him as a result. The actions of Jesus are clear evidence that the gospel is not inscribed on only one side of a coin. Life is holistic; therefore, any ministry should be as well.

I became convinced that it was time to stop the pendulum in dead center, to meet the spiritual, physical, social, and intellectual needs of the kids and their families in Orange Mound. As you'll see, this widening worldview didn't come into focus overnight. It was clearly time for a change, but how? For me, it all started with tutoring.

A Case for the Social Gospel

The first time I heard the term "social gospel" was in a warning that I was getting perilously close to it. I had begun to recruit tutors for the kids in our two Young Life clubs, the one in Orange Mound and another some volunteers started on the north side of town. I was taken to task for this activity because, presumably, it would blur my focus. I was told, "Young Life is committed to incarnational evangelism. We do that one-on-one, through club and camping. We disciple through our campaigner groups (Bible study). We don't' get involved in tutoring."

Talk about mixed messages. Growing up in my conservative evangelical church, we were constantly exposed to foreign missionaries who used the social services they provided as a platform for the gospel. I attribute my early stirrings toward ministry, in part, to my exposure to these men and women who were willing to put their faith on the line, many living near poverty levels, and most living among the people to whom they were called as missionaries. Nearly every one of them had started a school, opened a hospital, served as a medical missionary, or helped with agriculture. So it was strange to me that what I was doing in America was somehow not "evangelistic" and labeled a "social gospel," while missionaries overseas had often been holistic in their approach to mission. Why not in America? Why not in the inner city?

If holistic ministry overseas was acceptable, why couldn't I use it here to "get my foot in the door?" In others words, if you met a physical need like literacy, medical assistance, or hunger and thirst on the mission field, then you could "win the right" to speak about Jesus. If you examine this approach, you can't help but conclude that it was a sort of manipulation of people, what might be called "rice evangelism." That is, I'll give you rice to eat for your body if I can preach the gospel to your soul. Others refer to this as "needs-based" evangelism, meaning that if you meet felt needs first, you will "earn" the right to share the gospel at some point.

At the time, given my theological or missiological immaturity, I cast tutoring in that light. We tutored because it gave us the opportunity to really get to know the kids by meeting a "felt" need. I could justify coaching the baseball team that way, too. The school didn't have a qualified baseball coach, but a lot of the guys I was getting to know wanted a team, especially in the summer, something to break the boredom. So, by coaching, I had an entrée to their souls.

Friends of ours, Lewie Polk and Mack Oates, who were schoolteachers in an inner-city junior high on the north side of town wanted to start Young Life there. It was the same community where I would steal off and play basketball as a kid. So we started our second Young Life Urban club there, totally run by volunteer leadership, people I am close with to this day. One of those leaders and his wife relocated, too, so they could be close to the kids and held club at their house.

Young Life had this right: The basis of biblical faith is the incarnation. Jesus became one of us—mind, soul, body, and spirit—so that he could redeem us and make us fully whole—in mind, soul, body, and spirit. This ancient Jewish construct defines humanity. Jesus uttered the words, "Thy kingdom come, thy will be done, on earth as it is in heaven," in the same breath with a prayer for daily bread and forgiveness from sin. In his words, the very essence of the kingdom is holistic.

I believe that the theological paradigm of Western Christianity in which I was raised was more Greek than Hebrew, more Gnostic in its approach. Faith had to do with the spiritual. Salvation had to do with the soul, not the body. Sure, it was important to live moral lives in order to honor Christ in our outward behavior, but that's as far as it went. The implications of this incomplete theology are quite frightening. A conservative Christian could justify his own salvation and at the same time own and rent slums and take advantage of the poor because his "soul" was saved. The only behavioral mandates that mattered had to do with drinking, sex, abortion, homosexuality, and smoking—the more personal, private sins. Behavior toward the poor, or political activism on behalf of the oppressed, were not a part of those mandates. Only the spiritual really mattered. Racism, bigotry, and social injustice weren't considered personal sins or moral issues, and so they were not addressed by conservative Christianity.

This compartmentalization doesn't exist in the Hebrew worldview from which the scriptures were written. Holistic ministry touches the spirit, the mind, the body, the community in which one lives, institutions, all of life. So, while we preach to convert men and women to faith in Christ, we are equally committed to social justice on behalf of those who have no justice. We are as concerned about saving souls as we are about public education. We are as committed to the Great Commission as we are to the Great Commandment to love God and my neighbor as myself. We can't leap over the Great Commandment to get to the Great Commission, nor can we ignore the Great Commission in light of the Great Commandment. Both are essential for the disciples of Christ. We are as concerned about evangelism as we are about the context in which those we evangelize live.

Over time, it became clear that Christian discipleship could still resemble a wheel with Christ at the hub. But now there were more than four spokes. Added to Bible study, prayer, fellowship, and witnessing were compassion, service, mercy, and social justice. If any of the spokes were missing, then "the obedient Christian life" was not nearly as obedient as we once thought. The wheel would get out of balance, the tread on one side or the other wearing thin and finally becoming flat. And, of course, the horizontal and vertical dimensions of the Christian faith were not so neatly defined, either. Loving God, what we might call the vertical dimension of our faith, and loving my neighbor, what we might call the horizontal dimension, are so intertwined that to say, I "hate my brother" but "love the Lord" is an oxymoron, at least according to 1 John 4:20. If I can be a Bible scholar, meditating on his Word day and night and yet close my hand to the poor or discriminate against a person of color or not treat my employees justly, is that Christian maturity? No, it's a truncated gospel.

Holistic ministry holds the twin mandates of scripture, the Great Commission and the Great Commandment in tension. Or, as James put it in his epistle, "What good is it, my brothers, if a man claims to have faith but has no deeds? Can such faith save him? Suppose a brother or sister is without clothes and daily food. If one of you says to him, 'Go, I wish you well; keep warm and well fed,' but does nothing about his physical needs, what good is it?" (James 2:14-16, NIV) Tutoring and evangelism, then, are two sides of the same coin. Advocating for fair housing legislation and discipleship belong together. We dare not separate evangelism and discipleship from social justice and action on behalf of those who are marginalized or oppressed.

I understand the danger in this tension. It's easy to swing the pendulum toward social justice and forget the mandate of evangelism. Or we can just as easily err on the other side, leading people to faith with little concern for social justice. I contend, however, that the twentieth-century evangelicalism in which I was nurtured could condone racism, injustice, and horrors against the poor because of an anemic view of what the Bible says it means to follow Christ, because it adhered to a Western worldview rather than a Hebrew one. If all that matters is the soul, then we don't concern ourselves with the whole person or institutional sin and injustice.

In the Company of Rebels

Alan Hirsch, in his book *The Forgotten Ways*, says, "The challenge for the church and its leaders is to discern the will of God for our time addressed to it in the mouth of its holy rebels."[19] I'm not very holy, but I am a rebel. And I have had the privilege over the years of rubbing shoulders with plenty of the church's rebels who are far holier than I am.

About the time we started our tutoring program, I met two guys who were also doing work in the inner city: Jon, a white guy who worked with Youth Guidance, and Billy Joe,

---

19 Alan Hirsch, *The Forgotten Ways: Reactivating the Missional Church* (Grand Rapids: Brazos Press, 2009), 56.

an African American guy who was with Prison Fellowship. We'd grab lunch or breakfast together at a place near Memphis State University (now the University of Memphis) called the Varsity Inn and kick around theology, missiology, and strategies for our own ministries. We discovered that each of us was facing similar struggles in our organizations around this issue of holistic ministry, which, bottom line, amounted to issues of theology. These weren't just esoteric notions we had in our heads. We each interacted daily with kids or adults who got out of prison and couldn't find work. We each knew at least one kid who was going to school without breakfast or couldn't see the chalkboard because he had never been to an optometrist, or a kid who landed in juvenile court time after time.

The three of us became inseparable. We could share deeply and we understood one another. We each felt marginalized and misunderstood in our respective organizations. I believe that had it not been for this group and a few others, I would have failed, or worse, simply quit. Working in Young Life was a struggle, always filled with tension because urban ministry in Young Life was about change, and change is always difficult. What I was doing seemed like a threat to the organization. There was little support outside of other Young Life Urban staff in the early days. There was not much support for Jon or Billy Joe, either.

Jon, Billy Joe, and I decided over those lunches to encourage one another and work together. We began formulating what we eventually called a "collaborative" effort. People who work in the city are always collaborating.

Over the years, of course, the idea of collaboration has really caught on. You can't find a foundation out there that provides funding that won't ask who you are collaborating with. But to us at the time, it seemed like a novel idea.

While we had to get our own jobs done in our own

organizations, we each had similar challenges. None of us had sufficient volunteers to meet the social needs of the kids and adults in our ministries. At the time, there was no Christ-centered ministry in Memphis that provided emergency housing for families. There were few places for families seeking academic enrichment, rental assistance, legal help, or medical services. In other words, there was no Christ-centered, holistic, community-based ministry in Memphis. There was the Salvation Army, of course, and the Rescue Mission. But they had a clearly targeted audience, and youth were not in their sights at the time. We each had enough trouble finding a few volunteers for our own programs, much less for these other issues.

In the safe, inner sanctum of our time together, we started asking questions. What if we worked together and created a center in an under-resourced community that could meet all these needs in one place? What if we targeted a neighborhood? For example, if we pooled our talents, could we recruit, say, twenty volunteer tutors who would all come on Tuesday night? We'd train them, be there for support, get our kids to the center, make the center secure and safe, and sort of build a community of people who cared for the poor.

The three of us were meeting enough "evangelical" Christians who were committed to social justice like we were; others who had begun to question their own belief system that had no room for anything but evangelism and legalistic discipleship. They were reading their Bibles! But not everyone could lead a Young Life club. Let's face it, working with high school kids in the "inner city" is not for everyone. Nor is relocation. But almost anyone can tutor a kid, mentor a kid in trouble, find help for a family who has been evicted, or help out with Vacation Bible School in the summer. Anybody can be a friend. There was no institution in Memphis at the time with a "system" to utilize this growing population of volunteers who were simply dissatisfied with evangelical Christianity and the status quo.

So, our idea was to create that system. We found a church in North Memphis that was pretty much dead. The church building was in decent enough shape and it had a huge basement. The congregation was paltry. I don't even remember now if they had a pastor. But we were able use the basement of the church to start this collaborative experiment. Jon and his Youth Guidance staff moved their offices to the church and bore the brunt of the day-to-day responsibility of what was about to unfold. Most of the kids they were working with lived in North Memphis. We had a Young Life club in North Memphis, too. My home and ministry were in Orange Mound, which is more to the south and east, but I committed to getting my kids and their families to the north side for tutoring as we developed the ministry.

Our first initiative was a tutoring program. At this time, there was no formal organization, just three guys working together along with the Youth Guidance staff. I asked a woman named Debbie, a schoolteacher from the church where I had grown up, and her mother to head up the tutoring program. We had some pretty high expectations. We wanted a curriculum with workbooks. We wanted tutors who showed up trained and ready to do the job. We wanted it to be meaningful for the student and for the volunteer, so both would keep coming back. We wanted the student to do better in school, and we wanted the tutors to really get to know their kids. We wanted to break down barriers and stereotypes on both ends. Most of these volunteer tutors were white and many came from a couple of large suburban churches who had begun to be open at least to the idea of urban ministry and holistic expressions of the gospel. It wasn't long before we had dozens of tutors helping kids get ahead in school.

The next program was Vacation Bible School in the summer. So many of the kids around the center had very little to do after school was out. As a privileged kid, I was never bored in the summer. We took vacations. We had a little cabin at a lake about forty-five minutes from Memphis that we rented with four other families. I water-skied or went fishing almost every weekend. I played baseball and basketball in summer leagues. Summers were great for me. But in the inner city, about the only thing going was the local community center run by the Parks Commission, and not every community had one of these. My wife Becky and some of her friends ran the Vacation Bible School, driving around in our old van picking up kids and getting them to the center.

Unemployment was a huge issue, particularly with the men in Billy Joe's ministry who were being released from jail. No one wanted to hire them, yet without a way to earn a living, they would inevitably return to crime and be imprisoned again and again. We shared this with one of Jon's board members who, along with our help, started a job-training program for men at the center. We worked with a local business owner who manufactured storm windows and offered these men the opportunity to learn a trade and earn a living. This was a very successful program, so much so that our volunteer board member eventually sold his share of his own business to head up the governor's statewide program called Jobs for Tennessee Graduates.

We noticed that the families of many of our kids got caught up in legal problems, primarily contract disputes with a slum landlord from whom they rented their homes. Another one of Jon's friends, an attorney, agreed to pull together Christian attorneys and form our first Christian legal assistance program. Initially, we had a pretty good number of lawyers committed, but eventually this program proved to be too much. Contract disputes were one thing, but there were all kinds of other issues ranging from criminal justice to child support. In the end, the legal assistance program was disbanded.

It wasn't long before the center was bursting at the seams. Jon and his Youth Guidance staff were doing the heavy lifting since their offices were there. We decided that the center was successful enough to take the next step. We would incorporate it and find staff to run day-to-day operations and organize volunteers. Each of us was already working seven days a week and around the clock with our own ministries and volunteering countless hours in order to maintain operations at the center.

We decided on a name: The North Memphis Christian Center. We recruited a board of directors, beginning with a young attorney and an accountant. The two of them would be our incorporators and get us organized as a nonprofit corporation, really the first Christian community development corporation in Memphis, though we didn't know what one was! Then we expanded the board and recruited a group of young men and women who were becoming convinced that holistic, urban ministry was important in our city.

In the meantime, the center just kept growing. It was time to look for a director. We had no money for this fledgling corporation. Nor did we have any support from our respective organizations. We approached a local Presbyterian church from whom many of the center's volunteers had come, Second Presbyterian in Memphis, and asked them to consider a start-up grant so we could hire a director and get the center on firm footing. They agreed, and we received a grant of fifteen thousand dollars, a huge sum of money in 1978. The associate pastor at Second Presbyterian at the time also helped us recruit some key board members from the congregation. Our new chairman was Frank Fourmy. Frank served on the center's board as chairman for over ten years. He was a godly man and full of wisdom, exactly what we needed.

Jon and I were still pretty young. We were brash and full of ideas. Frank was older, wiser, and a great strategic thinker. Together we would make a great team.

Now it was time to find a full-time leader for this fledgling community development ministry. We had funds raised from Second Presbyterian. But we needed more funding to get this idea to scale, so we approached First Evangelical Church, the church where we had so many volunteers, and the very church where I had been raised. First, I met with one of the elders and the pastor for breakfast. I remember that day! It was a Saturday morning at Shoney's, the home of the Big Boy Hamburger in Midtown Memphis. It was a long breakfast. I sought to justify to these two men the absolute necessity of holistic ministry in the city. First Evangelical was somewhat famous for the vast number of missionaries she supported, many of whom had grown up in the church. Evangelism was her major focus. But most of that work was international in scope. Here was a chance to do something in our own city. We already had dozens of volunteers from this church, along with the tutoring coordinators who volunteered hours upon hours of time to the project. But this was new. We were pioneering a holistic, community-based ministry that certainly had evangelism as a primary focus, but also included education, legal assistance, job training, and much more.

I think we sat there till lunchtime. In the end, I was asked to make a presentation to the entire elder board about this idea. I gave pretty much the same spiel to the elders that I had given at the breakfast meeting. Lots of questions followed. In the end, First Evangelical also got on board, and matched the gift we got from the Presbyterians. Now we had funds to hire a director with some funds for programming, too.

I don't remember to this day how Jon and I ran across JoAnn Ballard's name. JoAnn was working in social services at another nonprofit in North Memphis when we met her.

We had lunch together and knew right away that we wanted to hire JoAnn as our director, and I believe we offered her a job on the spot. She was either gracious enough or foolish enough to help us with this vision and took the job. She was executive director of the Neighborhood Christian Centers (we changed the name soon after we incorporated, with the idea that other centers would follow, and we didn't want to incorporate them separately) until her retirement in 2008. About that time, Jon moved to Atlanta to work with Evangelicals for Social Action (ESA) and Billy Joe was reassigned to Nashville. So it was JoAnn and me, along with the Youth Guidance staff who still had offices at the center, and our newly formed, enthusiastic board.

The center really took off once we had the kind of vision and energy JoAnn brought to the table full time. The NCC now boasts seven neighborhood centers and close to fifty satellites that provide services across Memphis. Each year they serve thousands of our city's most desperate neighbors in the name of Christ, with a plethora of programs aimed at encouraging the poor to wholeness.

My role changed when we hired JoAnn. I was now on the board and the volunteer director of development, which is a fancy term for a fund-raiser. I was doing a fair amount of this with Young Life, too. The center flourished and grew beyond anything we had expected. We hired the first African American staff person in Memphis; in fact, the first black Young Life staff person in the mid-South region at the time. With this hire we expanded Young Life Urban and quickly hired an African American woman soon after, increasing our staff from one to three. During this time the synergy of these three organizations, Young Life, Neighborhood Christian Centers, and Youth Guidance, was a thing of beauty.

Sounds like smooth sailing, right? Well, if you know anything about pendulum swings and about the rebels who push the pendulum in the opposite direction, you may surmise that it wasn't all that smooth. And you would be right. Even more change was in the wind. Little did Becky or I know how drastic that change would be.

Whatcha gonna do?

1. Is your thinking more Greek than Hebrew in that you consider the physical and the spiritual completely separate?
2. Describe the basic pursuits of a holistic life and ministry.
3. So much ministry creativity emerges out of friendships like the ones I forged with Jon and Billy Joe. Are you engaged in friendships that encourage you toward redemptive action?

Chapter 6

Smart White Boy

Mentors and Other Kinds of Brothers

The mind is not a vessel to be filled, but a fire to be kindled.

—Plutarch

Only your real friends will tell you when your face is dirty.

—Sicilian Proverb

Your anger can never make things right in God's sight.

—James 1:20, NLT

I've always had a problem with anger. I guess you could say I had a short fuse. I'm not suggesting we should sin so that grace may abound, but you could also say God uses us even in our weakness.

Anger is not an event; it's more like a condition, a condition I most certainly have. From the beginning, my reaction to things that aren't right in the world has been anger. Becky says that there have been times when my anger about justice issues in the city frightened her. When I saw injustice, I just got mad. When I saw how our kids in the inner-city schools were receiving such an inferior education, it steamed me and still does. When I heard racist comments from other whites,

some of them friends, I just couldn't let them go unchal-
lenged. And I was becoming increasingly frustrated, then
angry, with my own organization for its lack of support for
urban ministry, not just in the Mid-South region, but across
the nation. I think we can all agree that there are times for
"righteous anger." But there were multiple times when my
anger was over the top, and rather than serving to enlist support from people, it pushed them the other direction.

The area director for Memphis Young Life resigned to
take a job at a local church that year. He had been very supportive of the urban ministry. He had hired me in 1975. The
search for a replacement began, and I thought I was the perfect candidate for the job. If I were area director of the city,
urban ministry would no longer be the "stepchild." And,
as we predicted then, Memphis City Schools would soon
be overwhelmingly African American and poor, as whites
kept fleeing the city and the public schools. I felt I had the
gifts and abilities for the area director's position. I was rais-
ing a lot of money for Young Life. I had dreams of leading
Memphis to become the first city in the nation where Young
Life was primarily focused on the city versus the suburbs,
where we could be an agent of justice, particularly in public
schools.

The regional director, however, had a very different idea.
In fact, nothing could have been further from his mind. There
were some very heated exchanges between the regional
director and me that year. Frankly, both of us had anger-
management issues. It came to a breaking point, and the
director of Urban Young Life, my mentor, Verley Sangster,
came to town to mediate. Reconciliation was out of the question at that point. I felt I had to leave Young Life Memphis,
and I began to look for other options.

In his most introspective and enigmatic book, Solomon
has this to say about life: "Notice the way God does things;

then fall into line. Don't fight the ways of God, for who can straighten out what he has made crooked?" (Ecclesiastes 7:13, NLT) Well, this certainly looked like a crooked place in the path to me. Even then, I wasn't sure who had created the detour, me or God. But, in the end, it's always God, isn't it? My inability to play nice, while not exemplary, was a flaw God used to get us to the next big thing. This certainly doesn't justify our misdirected actions. It's more grace than science. Even when we screw up, willingly or unwillingly, God doesn't write us off. He teaches us, guides us, and puts us back on his path…if we are willing to submit to him.

But first, a little more about anger. You may not be surprised that I was livid. I had been passed over for a job I felt I was more than qualified for. It's ironic, given the fact that I was a privileged white man living among people who—daily—experienced the injustice and ignominy of being passed over. For many of my friends and neighbors, injustice was a way of life. I will never experience it the way some people do—people of color or women, for instance—but I did get a taste of it then. We all know that the danger of anger lies not in the emotion itself, but in what we do with it. Here's what I did with mine: I held on to it for dear life.

Bitterness is a troublemaker. The writer of Hebrews warns against it: "See to it that no one fails to obtain the grace of God; that no "root of bitterness" springs up and causes trouble." (Hebrews 12:15, ESV) Back then, I would have said others were causing me trouble. What I didn't see was that the bitterness itself caused trouble. If Cain had heeded God's warning to wrestle the sin of bitterness, to "master it" or "rule over it" (Genesis 4:7), he would not have killed his brother, Abel. What I know now is that Satan took advantage of my circumstances and my own sinful reaction to get a foothold in my life. He was defeated on the cross, but he is still the biggest troublemaker of all, and there are times when, if we let him, it sure looks like he wins. I shudder to think where I'd be had the bitterness of that time continued to master me.

Mentors

You're probably reading this book for one of a handful of reasons. You live in Memphis or, wherever you live, you're doing research on community development or ministry in the city. Or someone gave you the book because you love your city. You're reading it for information, education, inspiration, or all three. And so maybe you're wondering what happened? Mentoring happened. Sometimes we need the sane people around us who love us no matter how off base we get to show us the way. A lot has been written lately about mentoring, and I agree that mentors are important pieces in the intricate puzzle of any organization, of any movement, any church. But I'll go a step further. Mentors are lifesavers. At least, that's what mine have been for me.

Fred

In 1976, I met Fred Davis, a businessman who lived in Orange Mound. Mr. Davis was one of the first African American city council members in Memphis. He was right in the middle of the historic sanitation strike. He chaired the committee that tried to negotiate a deal between the city and the sanitation workers to end the strike, the strike that brought Dr. King to Memphis. There's a famous picture of Dr. King leading the march in Memphis, and there, right next to him, is Fred. And I was going to meet him in order to get *him* to support Young Life in Orange Mound! The national director of Young Life Urban came from Chicago to meet him with Mr. Davis and Young Life Urban team. I was excited but totally intimidated.

Mr. Davis heard about my desire to start Young Life in

Orange Mound, or the "Mound" as many knew it. Of course, he had never heard of Young Life, since up to that time, Young Life didn't venture into his neighborhood or neighborhoods like his, at least not in most of the country. Young Life Urban was growing slowly, but primarily in the Northeast and Chicago. To my surprise, Mr. Davis not only embraced the concept but embraced me, literally holding my hand over the next several years as we developed the ministry. In fact, Mr. Davis has been my mentor ever since. I have never made a major ministry decision without talking it through with him first. He introduced me to pastors, business people, politicians, and school administrators. He even sponsored the first summer baseball team at the high school, a team that I coached. He bought the uniforms and paid the entry fees. We were the only black team in the American Legion summer league.

Fred Davis is in his eighties today. He's old enough to be my father. His wife Josephine or, "Jo" as he calls her, has stood by his side for over fifty years. She is a tiny woman with a huge intellect and passion for life. Fred is an independent insurance broker, one of the first African American brokers in Memphis. He grew up in the Jim Crow South. He attended segregated schools in Memphis. He grew up on the north side of the city and scraped his way through high school and then college. He attended Tennessee State, a historically black University where he and Jo met. He sent three kids to college. His insurance agency is in the heart of Orange Mound. He lives there, too, even though he could live anywhere in Memphis. He could have moved to the suburbs like so many others did. But he is committed to living out the gospel in his community.

Mr. Davis is a humble man. He is very soft spoken, so much so that you have to really listen when he talks. He has a wonderful sense of humor. When he gets to laughing, sometimes I think he's going to have a heart attack. His wisdom is incredible. He can dissect a difficult situation faster than anybody I've ever known, and he seldom makes mistakes. Nearly every major decision I've made has had Fred's thumbprint on it. The few times I didn't heed his advice were not pretty. He understands the value of letting his protégé fail. But, and here's the remarkable thing, he never pulled me aside, dressed me down and said, "I told you so." In fact, I don't think I've ever heard him put anyone down in the forty years I've known him.

More About Fred

Fred has received numerous accolades. He's a member of the Memphis Society of Entrepreneurs, as heady an organization there ever was; he was one of the first African American City councilmen and the first African American council member to win in a predominantly white district. He has served on many committees appointed by various mayors in our city. He has served on more boards of directors than I can name. He has received numerous awards, more than I can name, and I suspect, like many great but soft-spoken leaders, he will receive many more after he departs this earth and enjoys life with Jesus and all the saints who have preceded him.

If you were to look up "community servant" in a dictionary, I think you might find Fred's picture there. I, along with so many other young men he has mentored, often wonder how he could ever make a living. I guess Jo wondered that, too, from time to time. With as much time he has volunteered in our city and in his beloved Orange Mound, I don't know how he ever made a dime. But, if you asked him, he'd tell you that making a dime was just a means to an end. His primary goal was to love his neighbor.

Fred and I have a code language for our mentoring time. I'd call Fred and say, "Mr. Davis, I need some education." Then he'd laugh, and we'd get together for lunch or some time at his office so he could further "educate" me. I remember one day over an "educational" lunch in 1980 when I unloaded the unfair situation in which I found myself. Fred looked at me and said, "Welcome to the club!" He was trying to give me perspective, not minimize my feelings. He and other African Americans have been passed over, humiliated, discriminated against all their lives by the prevailing white culture, even in a city that was at that time 50 percent African American. He wasn't trying to be glib. He helped me understand that what had happened to me was an everyday occurrence for most people of color in a culture dominated by whites. Fred simply asked me what I was going to learn from the experience that would make me more useful for God's work. That was an important lunch. I had been letting my anger and resentment eat me up. One of the lessons learned is how we can grow to spiritual maturity by going through hardships, even hardships caused by us! God uses hardships in our lives, not to punish us, but to grow us. But we have to reflect on hardships, while in the middle of them and afterward, and consider how they have shaped us to be more and more like Christ, who himself was a "man of sorrows, associated with grief" (Isaiah 53:3).

Verley

In the 1970s, Young Life had no formal training to speak of for those of us who worked in the inner city. Training was the very thing I needed most. I met a man who later became the national director of Young Life Urban, Verley Sangster. He was doing Young Life on Chicago's West Side. We met first at a Young Life Urban conference I attended in the fall of 1976 in Pittsburgh. Man, was that a baptism! I was one of only a handful of white guys working with Young Life Urban at the time, and I was definitely the youngest at twenty-four. I remember one night late, a bunch of the staff guys were hanging out at the hotel. One of the veteran leaders (who was black), looked me in the eye and said something like, "We don't need any more white guys doing urban work... you won't last." How do you answer that? Then he asked me point-blank, "Why are you doing this?"

I can't remember exactly what I said, but it was something like "God has called me to this." He only smirked, and I did my best to disappear. Later, that veteran leader, Bill "Pee Wee" Winston, became one of my closest friends in Young Life.

At the conference Verley knew I was a rookie, intimidated and scared. He took me under his wing and invited me to Chicago anytime I wanted to "hang out" with him and learn the ropes. He became, from that day on, my second mentor, and he continues to play that role in my life to this day. I took him up on his offer, and I suppose I traveled by train to and from Chicago a half dozen times over the next few years learning everything I could from Verley and his team.

Originally from South Bend, Indiana, Verley moved with his family in 1975 to head up Young Life Urban on the West Side of the Windy City. He was thirty-six years old. He was immediately successful with young people and was great at youth evangelism. But I think his real gift is leadership development. He wasn't on the Young Life staff long before many of us began to look to him for leadership, not only in ministry but in "ministry life." He modeled the answers to the questions the ministry pushed to the surface in our lives: How do we balance urban youth ministry, which is a 24/7 job, with family life? How do we say "no" graciously? How do we rattle the corporate cage about justice in a way that can be heard?

Verley has a rare gift for developing deep relationships quickly. He is genuinely interested in people. In fact, he's a real student of people. He quickly finds out what makes someone tick. And his relationships span all sorts of racial and gender divides. He has deep and long-standing relationships with white, black, Latino, and Asian leaders, all over the world. He eventually began to call me a "Smart White Boy" or SWB, not necessarily because I'm all that smart, but because I was eager to learn from him and others. I still am.

More About Verley

After several years of "field staff" work on Chicago's West Side, Verley was tapped to be the vice president of urban ministry in Young Life. The Urban Primus Council of Young Life over which Verley presided asked him to become our leader at the national level. Bill "Pee Wee" Winston, the chairman of the council, and I, as vice chairman, were asked to visit with the president of Young Life and the national leadership team composed of divisional directors, to make our request for Verley's selection as vice president known. Young Life had had two prior VPs for urban ministry. Both were great men but with very little Young Life field experience. Verley was not only an exemplary servant leader, he understood the ins and outs of ministry on the streets with urban kids. And he had the relational skills needed to help Young Life National catch a vision for what we were doing in the cities of America. Our request for Verley's selection was taken into account, though it was made clear by the all-white male leadership of Young Life at the time that it was their decision, not the decision of the YL Urban staff, as to who would be selected. That meeting at the Navigators headquarters in Colorado Springs was a real eye-opener for Bill and me. . .well, probably more for me than for Bill. During those discussions, it was apparent to me that white leadership had little respect for anything other than, well, white leadership. The input of African American leadership was simply not important. To be sure, there were some divisional directors and even the president, Bob Mitchell, who valued what urban ministry was doing in Young Life, but there was a dearth of non-white leadership at the table.

Verley was eventually appointed as vice president, and Young Life Urban would see its best years under his leadership. Eventually, though, as is often the case, he, like many leaders of color, became marginalized over time. He resigned from Young Life as its vice president in 1993 and took on the job as president of the Center for Urban Theological Studies (CUTS) in Philadelphia, a ministry that partners with higher educational institutions to provide biblical/theological training for urban pastors in the city of Philadelphia. So many times, urban pastors have not had the opportunity to undertake formal theological training. CUTS makes it affordable, relevant, and convenient by bringing education to the pastors and "brokering" education with accredited colleges and universities.

Verley officially retired from CUTS twice! He had retired in 2004 but was asked to return after a failed presidency. He still consults with CUTS but has moved back to Denver, Colorado, where he and his beloved wife, Pearlean, can be close to many of their children and grandchildren.

Verley often called me to check in, so when he called in the fall of 1980, I wasn't surprised. In fact, I figured if ever I needed his wise, stabilizing influence, it was then. I had already decided I would leave Young Life, work for Neighborhood Christian Centers, and go to school part time to finish a master's degree I'd started at a local seminary in 1976. I actually enjoyed the heady atmosphere of academia.

It was a decent contingency plan, made in the wake of the disappointments of that year. I was all ready to pour out my sob story to Verley when he made me an offer that changed the trajectory of the next six years of my family's life.

Earlier that year, the Urban Primus Council on which I served had worked on a deal with Fuller Theological Seminary. They wanted to create an urban youth ministry curriculum, test it with African American pastors attending Fuller, and work with their churches in starting Young Life-type outreach ministries in the heart of the Los Angeles area. It was an exciting idea. At the time, though, the Young Life Urban staff person slated to be our representative was an African American who had served far more years than I had. Frankly, when we talked about the program at the council months earlier, it never crossed my mind that I would ever be in a position to be selected.

But then Verley called. The man slated for the job had decided not to go after all, and now the position was open. The program had been funded by the Lily Endowment out of Indianapolis, an endowment that had long been supporters of Young Life and Fuller. Verley wanted to know if I would consider going to represent Young Life in the program. He came to Memphis and stayed at our house to discuss this with Becky and me. The opportunity was perfect for me, given my decision to resign from Young Life in Memphis, anyway. But Southern California was a long way from home, especially when I had two children with both sets of grandparents and dozens of lifelong friends living in Memphis.

Becky, like me, had grown up in Memphis. We went to different junior high schools, both integrated. We met at Central High School, and I fell in love at first sight. I saw her for the first time in English class my first year at Central. I was smitten! When you grow up in a city and have a deep love for that city, when you embrace the theology of a place

and believe that God puts you in a place or city for His purpose, it is very difficult to leave. We both have friends to this
day whom we've known since elementary school, and a ton
more since high school. Relationships like those are precious,
and to leave them behind is painful.

Verley is a wise mentor. He knew that I wanted to do this
thing. But he also knew that Becky needed to make the final
decision. In an uncanny déjà vu, reminiscent of his advice to
me when I chomped at the bit to move to Orange Mound,
Verley instructed me to drop the topic and let Becky think
and pray it through. I knew this was a hard decision for her.
Making new friends on the other side of the country with
two small children isn't easy for anyone, even someone as
engaging as my wife. Leah was a little more than three, and
Lydia only a year old. I had been fully prepared to go to
seminary in Memphis and work for Neighborhood Christian
Centers as its fund-raiser. So, after he left, I never brought it
up again. I'd learned that Verley Sangster knew what he was
talking about.

A few weeks later, Becky came to me and said, "We need
to go to Fuller," and just like that we began planning our
move to California.

Whatcha gonna do?

1. Has your "righteous anger" ever gotten in the way of your ministry or relationships? How so?
2. Who are the mentors in your life? How has God used them to encourage and challenge you?
3. If you do not have a mentor, who might be a candidate, and how can you connect with him or her regularly?
4. Who are you mentoring? Each of us needs mentors, and we need to learn how to be a mentor to the next generation of leaders.

Chapter 7

West Coast Mentor

The evangelical community before God has the constant opportunity to be born again, to get into shape, to become everything it should and can be.[20]

—William Pannell

The best way to live in California is to be from somewhere else.

—Cormac McCarthy, in *No Country for Old Men*

And these God-chosen lives all around - what splendid friends they make!

—Psalm 16:3, MSG

Sometimes, in the pursuit of a clearly God-given goal, we have a moment when we wonder whether we're going in the right direction. Business guru Seth Godin calls it "the dip." It doesn't have to be anything rational, like downward market projections or a zoning board stalemate, or personal, like the advice of a well-meaning friend. Dramatic or subtle, conscious or not, it is that fleeting instant when what felt like

---

20 William E. Pannell, *The Coming Race Wars? A Cry for Reconciliation* (Grand Rapids: Zondervan, 1993), 128.

confidence edges toward doubt. For me, my first meeting with Bill Pannell was such a moment.

Dr. Pannell held the Chair for Evangelism at Fuller and administered the Black Pastors' program and the Urban Youth Initiative in partnership with Young Life Urban and Youth for Christ. It was an exciting initiative, and I was honored that Verley had asked me to represent Young Life. Rick Gray represented Youth for Christ. We were tasked with developing the curriculum and teaching the fundamentals of urban youth outreach ministry to pastors. We would also work with the pastors and their churches to develop outreach to unchurched teenagers in their communities. It was a two-year gig. If we were successful, the Lily Endowment would extend our grant for an additional two years.

I had read Dr. Pannell's book *My Friend, The Enemy*, and had heard him speak at a couple of conferences. I can think of no more gifted preacher than William Pannell, or "Doc," as everyone at Fuller called him. He was a deep thinker when it came to theology and mission, and deeper still when it came to justice and racial reconciliation. Doc was also on the national board of Youth for Christ and was 100 percent committed to youth ministry. He was passionate about mobilizing the church to do this work. I couldn't wait to meet him, get the preliminaries out of the way, and start work in the fall of 1981.

I flew the "red eye" into LA and caught a bus from the Los Angeles Airport to Pasadena where the seminary had arranged for a hotel room late that night. I had never been to California. Pasadena, the City of Roses, is just northeast of downtown LA and sits at the foothills of the San Gabriel Mountain Range. It is a lovely spot indeed. The Fuller campus in downtown Pasadena had lush green lawns, palm trees, and the whole Southern California mystique. It's not in any way an opulent campus, but it is a beautiful place. It would be our home for a number of years to come.

I awoke in proverbial sunny California the next morning and walked to the Fuller campus for our nine o'clock meeting. I arrived a little early. Dr. Pannell was on the phone, so I waited in an outer office with his assistant for a few minutes. And then it happened. Nothing dramatic, just a little pebble of doubt in my shoe. I'd been so excited to meet the man I considered a hero of justice, so ready to work with him, and so certain God was in this plan. I'd just assumed Dr. Pannell would feel the same way. Now, don't get me wrong, Doc is an amiable man and his demeanor that morning didn't stray from what I now know him to be. You will never meet a more outgoing, gracious, and genuine gentleman. But there was an undercurrent of tension in the air and I couldn't put my finger on exactly what it was. Or who caused it. We had a cordial enough conversation, and over the course of a couple hours he warmed up a bit but, still, something was amiss. Dr. Pannell was the gauntlet, one for whom I was not prepared to be anything but a welcome banner. I was still sure I was exactly where I was supposed to be, but I wondered a little. How was this going to work out if he didn't want me there?

He explained the program, told me that Rick Gray, my counterpart in Youth for Christ, would be coming the next day or so. He then turned me over to his assistant to work out details. For the next few days I arranged for student housing, filled out paperwork for entry into the school of theology seeking the Master of Divinity degree, met with an academic advisor, procured transcripts, and registered for the fall. It was like going back to college, only this time I got to study theology at one of the world's most renowned seminaries. The nagging doubt I'd felt in Dr. Pannell's office ebbed and all but disappeared. I was jazzed.

Mentoring, the Key to Success

Work in the inner city in those days, at least in Memphis and in many major cities, meant work in the African American community. This was not some romantic notion; it was simply the reality. I knew that if I was to be successful I had to learn from men like Verley, Fred, and the other men who eventually became my mentors and teachers: Bill Pannell, John Perkins, Bill Winston, and Bo Nixon, among others. In fact, over the years, I've noticed that there are a whole lot of white guys who want to "save" the city but are unwilling to follow black leadership. That's like learning concert violin without one lesson from an actual violinist. The result is typically a lot of screeching.

Verley, Fred, (and soon) Bill Pannell and John Perkins invested years of ministry wisdom in me. I have had the privilege of mentoring a lot of younger men, too. Some of these men have been white and others have been African American or Latino. I tell every one of them, especially the white guys, that one sure way of failing in urban ministry, especially if you're white, is thinking you have the answers. Heck, I didn't even know the questions! That's why mentoring is so crucial in our ministries. I can ask Verley, Bill, John, or Fred anything. They're not going to ridicule me, lecture me, or think badly of me. When I make mistakes, they put some salve on the wounds. There have been times throughout my career when I have failed, where I've been misunderstood, or made huge mistakes. They helped me pick up the pieces without ever once judging me.

Friend/noun/'frend:
One attached to another by affection or esteem [From the Old English frēon to love, frēo free] *(Merriam-Webster)*
Attached and *free? Aren't those antithetical terms?*

Every family has one: the crazy aunt, the weird uncle, the high-maintenance sister, the mother or father whose eccentricities or abuses require a sense of humor or distance or healing to endure. It is this kind of family member who must have inspired the familiar phrase: "You can choose your friends, but you can't choose your family." (Who knows, I may be the one in my family whom everyone has to put up with from time to time. You may be, too.)

But our friends, now they're another matter. Those are the attachments we make freely, by choice. Those are the relationships that fit us, like an article of clothing we purchase after trying several others on for size in the dressing room. Because choice is inherent in friendship, it's easy to conclude that we can pick and choose friends like clothing or ice cream flavors, according to our personal likes and dislikes. And we are free to do it that way... if we follow the culture instead of Christ.

Attached and free.

The love of Christ makes the paradox possible. He didn't have to, but he freely chose us, revealed his Father to us, and sacrificed his life for us. That free gift of friendship, when we accept it, means we are inextricably attached to him for life. It is a no-strings-attached offer that binds us to the Giver with cords of the love that offered it. His free gift gives us the pattern to follow.

Each of us needs to encourage younger men and women. It means so much when older leaders not only place a mantle of responsibility on younger men and women but become their cheerleaders as well as their coaches. For some, fathers and mothers play this role. My parents certainly did. This is wonderful, but our parents are "supposed" to be our fans, after all, or at least it should operate that way. However, we leaders should never assume that our charges are getting encouragement anywhere. Not everyone has been blessed to have parents who are on their side.

One of the greatest things we can do as mentors is to encourage those we mentor *instead of* giving advice. Advice is fine when it's solicited, but encouragement is worth much, much more. I arrived at Fuller because Verley believed in me. He still does. His confidence has been an incredible gift to Becky, the kids, and me over the years.

Pannell picked up the phone to call Verley that morning as soon as I left his office. Had I overheard that conversation, I would have understood the source of the tension I felt during our meeting. Seems Verley had neglected to tell Pannell that I was white! Understandably, he was shocked when a balding, bearded white guy walked into the interview that morning. He had assumed I would be black, which makes perfect sense. I'd be teaching African American pastors how to reach black youth in the inner city. He was taken aback and he sincerely wondered whether I would succeed. Verley told him, "Just you wait and see. He'll succeed. He's a Smart White Boy!"

I didn't hear about this conversation until years later. And I'm glad I didn't. Had either one of them told me, I may have been tentative in my work at Fuller, always wondering whether I met with Pannell's approval. In time, Pannell became a valuable mentor, so much so that he finally told me about the conversation he'd had with Verley that morning. As far as I could tell, he accepted me after our first meeting. He's my theological mentor these days. I'm sure he would fill bigger shoes in my life, just like Verley and Fred, if not for the nearly 2,000 miles between us. I have yet to meet a man more in tune with God's heart when it comes to mission in the city.

Each of my mentors has a role in my life. John Perkins was soon to become my mentor in community development. Pannell, as I've already stated, is my theological/biblical mentor. Fred is my business and social mentor. Verley is my ministry mentor. Each, from time to time, has also played the "personal mentor" role in issues like family or finances. Each of these men was farther down the road in every area of life. And yet they modeled the importance of both sides of the mentoring relationship. John wrote, "While it takes humility to learn, it takes real commitment and character on the part of mentors to guide. Both are learning experiences that can deeply shape our ministry skills and character."[21] No matter how old or experienced I become, I will never outgrow the need for mentors. And I will never cease to mentor younger men.

Life in the Foothills

It was time to hand off the baton of leadership in Memphis. But to whom? The two African American staff members I had hired in Memphis were pretty green at the time, and we ultimately lost both of them, one to work full time with Neighborhood Christian Centers and the other to another city. One of the suburban Young Life staffers, Eli Morris, had been a good friend of mine for years. In fact, we grew up in the same church. Eli led a club on the east side of the city that was largely suburban and white, though with busing, African Americans attended there as well. Ironically enough, the kids being bused "out there" were from Orange Mound. Eli was a brother all along. He was my biggest supporter on the area staff, and I, his. He understood the importance of cross-cultural relationships. Early on, his "campaigner group" of guys and my group in Orange Mound got together for fellowship, basketball, and study. We began to take these two groups together to Disney World in Orlando during

---

21 John M. Perkins, *Restoring At-Risk Communities: Doing it Together and Doing it Right* (Grand Rapids: Baker Books, 1996), 219.

Christmas break. This was a fruitful ministry for both groups of kids, and some deep friendships resulted.

I asked Eli if he would be interested in taking my place as the lead urban staff person and build on what we had started. He knew Young Life. He was ready for a bigger challenge and, unlike me, was a great diplomat. Eli agreed, and the transition couldn't have been smoother. He built on what we had started, increasing the staff and Young Life's outreach to other communities in the heart of the city. Eli also took my place on the Neighborhood Christian Center board.

With the ministry in Memphis in more than capable hands, we moved to the Foothills of California, an area that included Pasadena, San Marino, San Gabriel, and La Canada, all together over one million people. Each community had its own public school district, and there were far fewer private white schools than in the South. My daughter's first grade class was 30 percent black, 30 percent white, 30 percent Latino and 10 percent Asian. We loved living amidst such diversity. Pasadena was the "urban area" of the Foothills, with a higher percentage of minorities and poverty than the others. We eventually did Young Life work in Northwest Pasadena. John Perkins moved there in 1982. It was considered the "inner city" of the area. It was diverse as well, but it was primarily Latino and black.

In 1981, inflation had set in all over the nation, and interest rates for home mortgages were approaching 20 percent. There was no way we could sell our house in Orange Mound, so we rented the house to the mom of one of our "club kids." This "kid" later became my right-hand guy in ministry. We packed up a U-Haul, left some of our belongings in Orange Mound, and moved into a 600-square-foot student apartment on the campus. It was a remarkable place with students from around the world. Here we and our own kids befriended others from Africa, Korea, Australia, and other places far and wide. The majority of the international students in our student housing complex were from Korea and Africa. It was such a rich environment. And the weather! The song is right: It never rains in California. We could see the mountain range from our back door...that is, when the smog wasn't in the way.

After my first somewhat awkward meeting with Bill Pannell, I met with the Young Life team in the area. Young Life Urban in Pasadena was fairly healthy when it came to the ministry with kids. There were two urban clubs, one at Pasadena High School and one at John Muir High School. At first I served as a volunteer at Pasadena High, which became a platform to show pastors what youth outreach could look like in their own churches.

When classes started that fall I was in heaven. At Fuller, the first semester for the M.Div. students is intensive Greek: four hours a day, three days a week, with easily four hours a day of outside class work. We began developing the curriculum toward the end of the fall semester with implementation scheduled for the winter/spring semester.

In the meantime, Becky went to see a doctor because she thought she might be pregnant. Sure enough, she was. We already had two wonderful little girls in a tiny apartment and no money. We were paid a small stipend for the work at Fuller. We also got a scholarship for our tuition and books. That was it. By global standards, of course, that's a ton of money. Becky wasn't working. Keeping the girls, who were three and one, was a full-time job. I came home late one afternoon after she had been to the doctor's office, and there on the kitchen table were two ultrasound photos. I was thinking, that's nice we get two views of the baby. Wrong. We were having "Baby A" and "Baby B." Becky waited for my reaction. I was elated, I told her. Twins were a blessing from God. We knew we were in for some difficulties, not only financially but logistically. If we panicked, we just had to remember that the tiny apartments at Fuller seemed like mansions to our international friends.

I actually did fret about it, but I didn't see any reason to dampen Becky's spirit. Hers was the bigger challenge. Not only would she carry twins, but she would have the daily task of managing four kids under four years old.

Becky was placed on bed rest at the sixth month of her pregnancy. All the Fuller students, church and Young Life friends became our family. I'm not so sure we could have survived with all our wits about us without them. As soon as we discovered we were having twins, I went to Pannell and asked him if I could take on some other work in order to survive financially, and he agreed. We welcomed the twins into our busy world on June 1, 1982. The years 1982 to 1984 were a blur of activity!

John Perkins and What I Learned From Him

John Perkins moved to Pasadena in 1982, a year after we did. He bought a home not far from the house we eventually bought. John turned over his work in Mississippi to leaders he had mentored. Now he wanted to see if his idea of Christian community development could work in a sophisticated urban environment like Southern California. I got involved with him almost from the day he moved to Pasadena and have stayed connected to him and the movement he started, called the Christian Community Development Association, ever since.

When John got started in Northwest Pasadena, he held what he called "listening conferences." He simply invited the community to come and sit on his patio and share with one another what was good and what was not so good about their neighborhood. He asked them what they as a community could do to make the community a good place to live and raise a family. And then he listened. I learned a valuable lesson from these listening conferences. So many urban ministry types come into a community to "fix" the neighborhood. They are the so-called experts who are convinced they know what ought to be done. No matter that they are essentially outsiders who think they have a clear advantage over the insiders, the people who have lived their entire lives in the city. I've seen this time and again. In my early years of ministry, a successful white businessman approached me and wanted to "impact" an inner-city neighborhood. He saw a community "in need." Translation: in need of *his* involvement to make it better. When I asked how he knew what the community needed, I could tell he had never talked with anyone in the neighborhood. He simply formed an opinion based on his own perspective, an outsider's idea of a healthy community. He didn't know anyone in the community except me. Enlightened self-interest can certainly be a motivator. He wanted his business to thrive and he sincerely wanted to hire employees from the neighborhood. What I learned from John Perkins is that you have to listen to the community before you can be of any benefit to it. One tenet of effective community development is to realize that the people with the problem must come up with the solution themselves.

Every community has assets and deficits. It is a massive mistake to judge from a deficit perspective only. When we do, we miss all the incredible assets upon which a community can build. If you listen to people in the community you will hear about all those assets, and you will also hear, from their perspectives, what issues really need to be addressed. Members of the dominant white culture often see a situation and think they know what "those people" need. But it's really rather arrogant to swoop into a community, not as a learner, but as a self-appointed leader. What that self-appointed leader often fails to see is that every community has a host of leaders in its own right. Community development ministry seeks to empower these community leaders to improve their own community. A top-down approach to community development does not often yield sustainable changes. That approach can discount the ideas and aspirations of the very people "the helpers" may be trying to help. In fact, that kind of help can often do more harm than good.

Paternalism is a form of racism that assumes a superior status and imputes an inferior status to the "race" that it purports to "help." The mantra of the paternalist is, "They can't fend for themselves; we must help them and guide them." It's not explicit, but it's palpable. It's sort of like benevolent racism, really. But it is as devastating and crippling as the overt form of racism reflected in slavery or Jim Crow laws or a KKK rally. It is demeaning and it persistently ignores or even denies value and dignity to the people who are treated in this way.

John Perkins founded the Christian Community Development Association in the early 1990s. Ever the collaborator, John didn't just use his own work in Mississippi as a template for CCDA. He drew from the work of his disciples, Wayne Gordon and the late Glen Kehrein, in Chicago, and from the experience of a host of others. It was and still is a grassroots effort at developing community, a fact which stands in stark contrast to the top-down approach utilized by government and most other human services organizations.

In urban ministry, to be effective in a neighborhood, an inner city neighborhood, you've got to be involved at the grassroots level. Or, if you prefer a biblical term, at an incarnational level.

If we've learned anything from failed government programs, it's that top-down policies that ignore grassroots concerns and leadership lack perceptivity and foresight.

Take, for instance, Aid to Families with Dependent Children (AFDC). Who came up with that idea? AFDC often aided only in the breakup of poor families, both black and white. It was not based on free enterprise or self-determination or the dignity of persons created in God's image. AFDC did not reward integrity, hard work, or entrepreneurship. It did just the opposite. I'm not necessarily one for conspiracy theories. But, if I wanted to develop a system that would paralyze poor people, break up the family, and punish industry, I'd form something exactly like AFDC. We may chalk up AFDC and other "poverty programs" like it that did more harm than good to the "law of unintended consequences." The end product has caused generations of dependency.

Our culture is riddled with this kind of "institutional" racism and paternalism. Even after I moved into the "hood" in Orange Mound, all I knew was that the injustices made me angry. I was oblivious to the greater story until I began to study our culture. My time in California, and specifically my friendship with John Perkins and Bill Pannell, helped me to see more clearly, to think more lucidly, and, ultimately, to plan for the future with more hope for the city. I confess, and maybe you will, too, that when we look at our cities or communities that are poverty stricken, we can lose hope. The problems seem so big, so complex. We can be tempted to give up. But what we can learn from John Perkins and William Pannell and so many others is that we can make a difference if we listen to the community, listen to the poor, and begin working in tandem to realize their own aspirations. Big government programs, even big nonprofit programs come and go, often leaving behind carnage when they are de-funded, because the changes have been made from the top down instead of the inside out. Bob Lupton in Atlanta wrote a book called *Toxic Charity*, in which he discusses the idea of how charity can actually hurt rather than help. Bob is one of the champions of Christian community development and has spent a lifetime learning this lesson. The time we spent in Pasadena was a turning point in how to see the city...how to work with urban leaders in partnership so as to realize God's agenda for the community.

Whatcha gonna do?

1. Have you had moments when you wondered whether you were going in the right direction? What happened to get you back on track?
2. How is paternalism a destructive form of racism? Where do you see it played out in your city today?
3. How can you love others without being paternalistic toward them?
4. As you look at your own life, have there been times when your charity actually did more harm than good? Or, as you look at what your church does at Christmas and Thanksgiving or on mission trips, do you think people are ultimately being helped or hurt?
5. How can you turn the events mentioned in Question 4 into development or empowerment events?

Chapter 8
Two Cultures Collide

The city has always functioned like the woofer and tweeter of an amplifying system.[22]

—Ray Bakke

It's so easy for a kid to join a gang, to do drugs...
we should make it that easy to be involved in football and academics.

—Snoop Dogg

Of course teenagers can get rowdy. In Memphis and in Pasadena, a modicum of mayhem at our Young Life club meetings was a good thing; it meant the kids were engaged, having fun, and felt free to be themselves. But, as any leader, teacher, or parent knows, all is lost if the fun crosses that invisible line and things gets out of hand. In Memphis, I had an ace up my sleeve that quieted things down every single time. It worked like a charm.

All I had to do was stand up and say, "Let's pray."

Or, at the beginning of a talk: "Open your Bibles."

---

22 Ray Bakke, *A Theology As Big As the City*, 157.

In Memphis in the early 1980s, kids knew "how to act in church," whether they knew the gospel or not. The Christian worldview was woven into the culture so tightly that it influenced behavior, especially in the African American community. I've already discussed the ways this cultural expression of Christianity was often a problem, wooing people away from the pure gospel to a far lesser substitute. But it gave kids a reference point, so that they at least recognized the pivotal stories in the scriptures.

California, for me, was a harbinger of the post-Christian culture that made its way to Memphis not long after we returned. One night after a meeting of our Young Life club in Pasadena, I had an encounter with one of the kids that shocked me. I had just given a talk on Calvary, outlining in very simple terms the story of Christ's death on the cross. I had gotten to know this kid pretty well, so when I dropped him off at his home, I asked him if he wanted to give his life to Christ. As he stepped out of the van, he looked me in the eye with a confused expression on his face and said, "I have *never* heard that story you told tonight."

Not only was this kid un-churched, the Christian message was not even part of his vocabulary, much less his worldview. We were in a city where an overarching knowledge of Christianity was fast disappearing. It was the epitome of the "secular city," or the "Babylon" John describes in Revelation. And the kids reflected this godless culture in ways that trumped anything I'd seen in Memphis thus far. Some of the kids in my Young Life clubs were "gang bangers," members of the Crips or Bloods or the many newcomer gangs that were flooding into the cities of the Foothills

Some were just "wannabes," not really gang members but acting like them. Crack cocaine had hit the streets and the easy money it produced generated more violence and power among the gangs. Young kids would "sling rock" (sell Crack)

for the older guys. If they got caught, they merely spent some time in a juvenile facility rather than a longer stint in the adult jail. Crack was easy to dispose of in the event of a surprise raid. This was all new to me then, even though I had worked in the toughest areas of Memphis. But today this scenario could describe what goes on in Memphis as well. Cities are like that. They amplify culture so that it reaches beyond the limits of one city to others, making short work of the distance between.

This is a much bigger issue than I can address in a chapter that is, for the most part, about how Fuller's Black Pastors' Program connected area pastors with the youth in their community. What I saw in a city that prefigured the Memphis to come surely influenced how I would interact with my city in the future. Many of these kids were becoming hardened criminals before our eyes, and quickly demonized by the broader culture. That fact not only drove me to teach churches and pastors to reach them, it opened my eyes to the complexities of their issues, issues that festered into huge social problems. I was beginning to see the city in all its unholy glory. As Ray Bakke says:

> *Our cities are full of dens of iniquity. Our culture is described as essentially post-Christian, secular and often antithetical to biblical values and hostile to biblical virtue. Evil is multiplying, and the poor are increasingly in double jeopardy. To borrow again the language of Hong Kong minister Raymond Fung, "The poor are not only sinners; most often they are also the sinned against."*[23]

Forgetting

The beauty of both Young Life and Youth for Christ's approach to ministry is its simplicity. Incarnation: befriend

---

23 Bakke, *A Theology As Big As the City*, 108.

kids and share the gospel. In the spring of 1982, we began the youth outreach training portion of the Black Pastors' program with the goal of teaching this simple method to church leaders. Just as Christ became flesh and dwelled among us, we would incarnate the gospel. Rather than expecting kids to flock to our churches, we would go to them, meeting them on their turf. Eventually, we would disciple the kids who came to faith to do "teen-to-teen" evangelism. Our entire curriculum for pastors was developed around these concepts. By the end of our first semester, the pastors were eager to take what they'd learned in the classroom at Fuller back to their congregations, to implement the strategies built on the basic idea of incarnational evangelism. Our original goal was to help ten pastors begin full-blown youth outreach programs in their neighborhoods.

That's when the real obstacle course began. First, the churches had no youth ministry staff. In fact, the pastor was often the only full-time staff, and many of them were bi- or even tri-vocational. Not only were they caring for every member of their flock from the youngest to the oldest, they were juggling family concerns and another job or two as well. Second—and this is the biggest obstacle to youth outreach in any church in any city—once the un-churched kids began coming to their churches, the rank and file did not eagerly accept them. This wasn't Memphis where kids instinctively knew how to behave when the Bibles were opened or the choir sang. Talk about tension. The only way to describe the collision of these two diametrically opposed cultures is *messy*.

It seems to me churches are awfully forgetful. First, we forget the foundation upon which we were built. The churches Paul planted—the ancestral prototypes of our local churches today—were made up largely of Gentiles who had only recently exited paganism. The early Christians left cultures rife with polytheism, temple prostitution, and other despicable practices related to idolatry. Their entrance into the local Body of Christ surely prompted more questions than embraces. How would these pagans conform to the moral and ethical mandates of the gospel and of the Judaism in which the church was rooted? Would they corrupt the church? When street-wise kids come to church, people ask similar questions, questions that keep us from engaging or, deeper still, loving them. But aren't these questions answered in our forebears' struggles with the same issues as documented in the New Testament?

Apparently, the church fathers were not only comfortable with welcoming former pagans into their midst, they felt it unnecessary to "burden" them with a heavy weight of controls on their behavior. Note the shortage of rules handed down to the early church in a letter sent by the Jerusalem Council to the first churches: "For it has seemed good to the Holy Spirit and to us to lay on you no greater burden than these requirements: that you abstain from what has been sacrificed to idols, and from blood, and from what has been strangled, and from sexual immorality. If you keep yourselves from these, you will do well." (Acts 15:28-29, ESV) Clearly, the early church was founded upon grace, a grace that encircled the former pagans as well as the Jews, and not on rules: "But we believe that we will be saved through the grace of the Lord Jesus, just as they will." (Acts 15:11, ESV)

People in churches also forget where we, ourselves, came from. In his letter to the Ephesians, Paul reminds us:

It wasn't so long ago that you were mired in that old stagnant life of sin. You let the world, which doesn't know the first thing about living, tell you how to live. You filled your lungs with polluted unbelief, and then exhaled disobedience. We all did it, all of us doing what we felt like doing, when we felt like doing it, all of us in the same boat. It's a wonder God didn't

lose his temper and do away with the whole lot of us. Instead,
immense in mercy and with an incredible love, he embraced
us. He took our sin-dead lives and made us alive in Christ.
He did all this on his own, with no help from us!
(Ephesians 2:1-5, MSG)

Before coming to Christ, we were exactly where the most hardened gang kid is today. Yet, faced with that kid, that vivid reminder of our own sin, we forget that we were "all of us in the same boat" and we recoil. In doing so, we lose the opportunity to reach that kid with the gospel, the only means of escape for him...and for us.

I will never forget the time one of the church groups I was working with in the program joined us at a Young Life camp. Camping is a venerated tradition in Young Life's ministry to kids, and I had already experienced this powerful strategy to reach young people both in Memphis and in Southern California. Getting them away from the distractions of life and into God's creation does wonders for their receptivity to the gospel. In Memphis, a Youth for Christ staff person and I took our kids rock climbing and rappelling. We slept on hard ground under tents and shivered in the cold. We discovered that a young person can learn more about trust and faith when he's dangling at the end of a rope than when he's sitting in someone's basement listening to a talk. The camp outside San Diego was beautiful. We took kids from the community and volunteer leaders from their neighborhood church. We had personally trained this group and felt good about them. Their pastor was supportive. The first day's activities included group competitions and free time, both involving the pool. A female volunteer pulled us aside and informed us that "mixed bathing" was taboo—the boys and girls could not swim together. I had not anticipated this at all. There was no way we could pull that off! All weekend the ladies from this congregation, whose very purpose for being there was to be involved with the girls they brought, wore dresses (they weren't allowed to wear pants) and never put on sneakers. Furthermore, they informed us, they considered all the fun and games pure foolishness. We should simply sit the kids down and tell them about Jesus and the Holy Spirit and that they were headed straight to hell if they didn't accept him and live a life of holiness.

The neighborhood this particular church was located in was a hotbed of gang activity. How were they ever going to reach those kids if they had to become "holy" first? I had many long conversations with the pastor who became a good friend and colleague. He understood the need to reach the kids incarnationally, and he wasn't bothered by the messiness that would surely ensue if he actually engaged them. The problem was his congregation. Although a part of the "holiness" tradition, it was comprised of people who had come to faith from the same backgrounds as the "unholy" kids in their neighborhood. How quickly we forget where we come from.

Relational, Not Programmatic

It occurred to us that we had to train pastors in a new paradigm of church, to teach them to incorporate a spirit of outreach to youth who were outside the walls of their churches. We weren't the only ones to hammer home this outward-focused approach to ministry. The pastors heard it in their regular studies at Fuller. I do not envy local pastors. Their jobs are overwhelming as it is, so I understand that introducing something new takes time. I'm happy to say the pastors in our program were fast learners.

We continually made a distinction between program-centered youth ministry and the vastly different

incarnational-centered approach. In the former style of ministry, we set up a program, like, say, the Boy Scouts, and invite
people to participate. If they come, great, we have a program.
If not, then that program is a failure. The problem with this
kind of ministry is that it relies heavily on our ability to com-
pete with the entertainment available to kids today. That's
a battle we'll lose before we start, especially in Southern
California. Kids have options for their time 24/7. They don't
need another program. What they need are relationships.

Despite some resistance, we did succeed in a number of
churches, even a few of the "holiness" ones where the congre-
gants had the biggest theological and missiological hurdle to
jump over if they were going to incarnate the gospel in their
environments. Once they saw the need, they became convinced
someone needed to reach the kids. The problem was, and
remains today, that many are less than willing to do it themselves. They would much rather establish or fund a program,
because programs are easier and less messy than building relationships. Bottom line, they would rather someone else win the
kids over, but that someone was often the gangs.

Mass Evangelism

*By emphasizing incarnational, or relational evangelism, I am
not discounting mass evangelism. There is certainly a place
for that. But even mass evangelism is, at its core, relational
to some degree. If you've ever been a part of a Billy Graham
crusade, you know this is true. The big event at the arena
is the result of relationships built in the community. That's
why people come in the first place. And the follow-up, if it is
effective, is relational as well. Likewise, programs have their
place, but to do effective urban youth ministry, the program
must always be secondary to the relationships. Programs are
only platforms for relationship building.*

Another Two Years and Beyond

The Lily Endowment evaluated what we were doing and gave us two more years. Because I wasn't counting on that, I had already finished my M.Div. degree. Memphis was calling. But we weren't quite finished in California. This idea of mobilizing the Church to reach kids was just getting traction. We had to take it further.

It was during these years that I began struggling with my role in Young Life. Could we be more effective in mobilizing urban churches to do incarnational ministry, thus paving the way for kids to be folded into the church family? Would the churches we were working with fully embrace such a paradigm? And, could younger guys who were indigenous to the communities we served do much better work than I could? Why not engage and equip these leaders? Wouldn't this be more effective, more inside out than top down? I went to Pannell and asked for his advice. He suggested that my greatest contribution to urban ministry might not be as a Young Life leader in an urban club but rather as someone who empowered indigenous leaders to do what I was doing. Bam...he perfectly articulated what I was struggling with. He reminded me that I was part of the dominant culture, which gave me a platform to help the evangelical and white Christian community better understand the urban context. He broke it down into two choices: lead one or two Young Life clubs or train and fund hundreds of indigenous leaders to do incarnational urban ministry. He asked, "Which would have the greatest impact?"

That question, and the subsequent answer, re-set the trajectory of my life and ministry. When the Lily program officially ended in 1985, we kept it going through the support of Fuller, Young Life, and a new relationship we'd formed with

World Vision. We were able to hire three new staff persons to spearhead new Young Life clubs with urban churches in their settings. These Young Life staffers were doing outreach from their churches.

The Gospel

The California chapter of the story wouldn't be complete without a nod to Pam Trask, the co-area director with Young Life in Pasadena. Pam had been one of my YL kids in Memphis years before when I was a college volunteer leader. We operated as co-directors, all along planning for her to become area director when I left. Her direct ministry was to the suburban schools, while I focused on the urban areas. She became concerned for the "parking lot kids" in her wealthy suburban high schools, the kids who were *not* the jocks, cheerleaders, or student government leaders. These kids were into heavy metal, Goth, punk rock, and drugs. They were the outcasts of their insulated society, marginalized within their own culture.

A hidden message often found in Young Life jargon was "reach the key kids," which meant the popular, attractive, got-it-all-together kids. The thought was if we reached them, they would act as catalysts to reach others. If you went after the winners you would certainly have a successful club. The traditional suburban Young Life club didn't have a strategy to reach the parking lot kids. But Pam sure did. Amid similar challenges to urban ministry—winning trust, primarily— Pam rescripted Young Life. . . and made some people very uncomfortable in the process.

Like Bill Pannell, John Perkins, Verley Sangster, and Fred Davis, Pam modeled an approach to ministry that closely resembled that of Jesus. She was yet another reminder that the gospel doesn't follow our rules. When Peter, James, and

John stood before the Sanhedrin, it was obvious to their questioners that they were "uneducated, common men," (Acts 4:13, ESV) anything but "key" in their society. Yet Jesus chose them. In those days, Jewish boys memorized the Torah, the first five books of the Old Testament. The most ambitious worked toward mastering the entire Old Testament. Those who were recognized as the top of their class, the best and brightest, would then become disciples of a rabbi and "follow him." If a young man didn't make the grade, he learned a trade instead, often his father's. The majority of young men fell into this class.

By contrast, Jesus's approach to choosing his disciples looked haphazard and even ill-advised. Peter, James, and John were working their fathers' trades, either because they weren't educated or affluent enough to garner the attention of a rabbi. Matthew was an outcast. And, of course, they were from the Galilee of the Gentiles. Simon the Zealot was perhaps a former terrorist. Jesus chose ordinary people. He didn't choose the brilliant, the cultural icons, or those with any noteworthy accomplishments. And what about Paul? Who would have picked him to be the leader of the gospel mission to the Gentiles? Jesus would. And he still chooses men and women today who are more often than not the least of the least, not the best of the best. Sure, there are bright, gifted people who respond to the gospel and lead, but God often uses ordinary pots of clay to get the job done. Clay pots like you and me. Paul reminded the Corinthians of this when he wrote, "For consider your calling, brothers: not many of you were wise according to worldly standards, not many were powerful, not many were of noble birth." (I Corinthians 1:26, ESV)

But we persist in believing the myth that the world's resources, its wealth and knowledge and power, are the tools God prefers to use. In the musical *Fiddler on the Roof*, Tevye sings "If I Were a Rich Man," with its catchy, iconoclastic chorus. The song endures because its themes are so relatable, its longing so universal. It equates monetary wealth with well-being and wisdom:

> The most important men in town would come to fawn on me!
> They would ask me to advise them,
> Like a Solomon the Wise.
> "If you please, Reb Tevye..."
> "Pardon me, Reb Tevye..."
> Posing problems that would cross a rabbi's eyes!
> And it won't make one bit of difference if I answer right or wrong.
> When you're rich, they think you really know!

I was beginning to realize that the "needy" people in our cities possess the gifts, abilities, and ingenuity to transform their own communities. My job was to empower leadership, not necessarily to lead. This isn't just an egalitarian idea, at its core it is a gospel idea.

Whatcha gonna do?

1. How does your particular city amplify culture?
2. How can you, your church, or organization incarnate the gospel in your context?
3. What traditions or prejudices get in the way of incarnational ministry?
4. What gifts and innate resources do the "poor" in your community possess? How can you celebrate these and encourage their use?

Chapter 9

Who Moved My Label?

You can't be evangelical and associate yourself with Jesus and what he says about the poor and just have no other domestic concerns than tax cuts for wealthy people.

—Jim Wallis

I think it goes back to the fact that the evangelical community often does not have a biblical vision of God.

—Tony Campolo

Before moving on, let's take a look at a familiar label: Evangelical. It's important at this stage in the story, because in the next part of our journey we began to bump up against labels. As labels go, "Evangelical" can be far more misleading than accurate, but I'll go ahead and admit that I am one. If, that is, an Evangelical is someone who believes that the Bible is God's infallible, true Word, and seeks to live out what it says. Tony Campolo says: If the evangelical community became more biblical, everything would change. Most of us would probably agree with that. But I'm not sure we'd all agree about what "biblical" means. Labels, they can be troublesome.

Evangelical theology holds that God is the creator of all that is, that he is sovereign, that he exists as one God in three persons, that the Incarnation was literal, that Jesus came in the flesh as very God of very God, yet as man, and that through his atoning death on the cross, an historical event, we can be forgiven of our sins, sins that define every human being who ever lived, and through faith in Jesus Christ we find forgiveness and reconciliation with God and eternal life. We believe in the literal resurrection of Jesus, that he now sits at God's right hand and will judge the world in the future. We believe that we are saved by grace through faith, that we cannot be good enough or in any way earn our salvation. And we believe that the Holy Scriptures are inspired by God and our only authority for faith and the practice of that faith.

At its core, Evangelicalism is centered upon the gospel and the authority of Scripture. And if we lived out this gospel, "everything would change," right? But what if somewhere along the way Evangelicalism got redefined? What if Evangelicalism, because of our cultural captivity was stolen away and used to promote far lesser agendas than the sacrificial, incarnational, transformational, prophetic, and radical life of Jesus and his followers? A.W. Tozer wondered, "Is the Christianity of American Evangelicalism the same as that of the first century?"[24] Over fifty years later I wonder, too. Tozer observed that the gospel had been cheapened in his day into a consumer product, one that had many benefits and very few responsibilities:

> . . . the cross of popular Evangelicalism is not the cross of the New Testament. It is, rather, a new bright ornament upon the bosom of a self-assured and carnal Christianity whose hands are indeed the hands of Abel, but whose voice is the voice of Cain. The old cross slew men; the new cross entertains them.

---

24 A. W. Tozer, *The Best of A.W. Tozer, Book Two* (Camp Hill, PA: WingSpread Publishers, 2007), 87.

*The old cross condemned; the new cross amuses. The old
cross destroyed confidence in the flesh; the new cross encour-
ages it. The old cross brought tears and blood; the new cross
brings laughter. The flesh, smiling and confident, preaches
and sings about the cross; before the cross it bows and toward
the cross it points with carefully staged histrionics—but
upon that cross it will not die, and the reproach of that cross
it stubbornly refuses to bear.*[25]

This diminishing of the gospel is unacceptable and has
opened the door for so called Evangelicalism to become more
a pawn of political conservatives than it is good news for the
poor. The biblical mandates about seeking justice, releasing
the captives, or welcoming the stranger are often overlooked
in favor of an ever-increasing focus on the eradicating of
all threats to the "moral majority." Think I'm kidding? Just
observe what a leader of the "Moral Majority" has to say
below. He equates "discrimination" against "Evangelicals"
with the genocide of the Jews, or American slavery:

*Just like what Nazi Germany did to the Jews, so liberal
America is now doing to the evangelical Christians. It's
no different. It is the same thing. It is happening all over
again. It is the Democratic Congress, the liberal-based media
and the homosexuals who want to destroy the Christians.
Wholesale abuse and discrimination and the worst bigotry
directed toward any group in America today. More terrible
than anything suffered by any minority in history.*[26]

This quote would be laughable except that it is taken so
seriously! In the 1970s, when I began to read the Bible without
looking at it through my middle-class American lens, I sensed

---

25 Tozer, 119.

26 Pat Robertson, in a 1993 interview with Molly Ivins.

for the first time the revolutionary elixir of the gospels. Jesus is no friend of those who are not friends to the poor, the widow, the orphan, and the refugee. Evangelicalism had "spiritual-ized" the Bible, ignoring the clear, holistic directives that include feeding the poor, clothing the naked, and confront-ing injustice. In a word, if we're not careful, Evangelicalism may just embrace a twenty-first century Gnosticism, just like it did in the first seven decades of the twentieth century. We are in danger of once again relegating "being Christian" to a set of certain behaviors or positions on certain issues, or belonging to a particular political party, becoming known for what we are against, rather than what we are for. We may lose sight of the fact that the gospel is extremely "social" while at the same time deeply "personal." We must continue to be in the middle of the tug-of-war between a gospel defined in merely personal and spiritual terms and a gospel that is only concerned with societal reform.

In the 1980s, the abortion issue became a rallying cry for conservative or evangelical Christians at Fuller and in other parts of the country. Eventually, other issues became its pet flash points. Homosexuality and same-sex marriage are hot buttons today, while racism, injustice, the deplorable condi-tions of inner-city public education, slumlords, public housing policies, inadequate health care, and genocide in Third World countries get short shrift on many Evangelicals' agendas. It seems to me, after a cursory reading of scripture, that more is said in God's Word about injustice toward the marginalized than is said about many of the pet issues of the religious right.

I prefer the term "Christ-centered" or "follower of Jesus" to Evangelical these days. By that I mean that we are people who follow the Jesus of history, the Jesus of scripture, and are seeking to allow him, through the work and indwelling of the Holy Spirit and God's Word, to conform our lives to his so that we, the church, are empowered to transform our world. Christ cannot be high-jacked by Republicans, Democrats, or the so-called Moral Majority. He sits in judgment of them all. He is the King of Kings and Lord of Lords. He will not be co-opted even if his people often are. He stands above all cultures and judges them. We do not judge him. He judges us. It couldn't be any clearer that his absolute standards are justice and mercy: "He has told you, O man, what is good; and what does the LORD require of you but to do justice, and to love kindness, and to walk humbly with your God?" (Micah 6:8, ESV) The question I must then ask myself as a follower of Jesus is, "Am I actively seeking justice and mercy, and am I walking humbly with my God?" Frankly, I am not there yet. Not even close! Every day we stand before God and plead with him once again to make us more like Christ, more compassionate, more merciful, more forgiving, more just.[27]

Back to Memphis

Sometimes so-called visionaries can be blind. Sure, they may see something way out there on the horizon that no one else can see, but there are times when they don't see what everyone else can see, the thing that is right under their noses.

By the end of 1985, I was restless again. I'm not sure the title visionary fits me all that well, but one quality of a visionary that can crop up if they're not careful is discontentment, a general propensity to continually be on the lookout for the "next thing." But I believe God can stir up a sort of "sanctified impatience," a holy cattle prod, if you will. A good friend from Memphis, Craig Strickland, came to Fuller to complete his doctorate and, more than once, I unloaded some of my thoughts on him.

---

27 And I am sure of this, that he who began a good work in you will bring it to completion at the day of Jesus Christ. (Philippians 1:6, ESV)

Craig Strickland is the founding pastor of Hope Presbyterian in Memphis. Hope is a member of the Evangelical Presbyterian Church. When Craig visited us in California, he was the executive pastor of Second Presbyterian Church in Memphis, the first church that helped us get the Neighborhood Christian Centers started in the late 1970s. Hope is the largest church in the denomination and one of the largest in the country. From the beginning, Hope Presbyterian was committed to ministry in the city. It's part of her DNA and in large part due to Craig's vision and leadership over the years. Hope started a Christian community development corporation in the heart of one of Memphis's most depressed neighborhoods. Hope supports numerous urban ministries and each year hosts two "urban plunges," when Hope members spend four days in the heart of Memphis learning firsthand about our city's joys and pains. Literally thousands of Hope members volunteer in city ministry each year.

How could I use my experience and knowledge to empower and equip indigenous leaders for the work of the gospel in the city? I was doing that in part with the Fuller Urban Youth program with African American pastors and through Young Life, but it seemed inadequate. And, while I was passionate about youth ministry and still am, I felt a need to embrace the whole city in addition to at-risk youth. I mean, so-called at-risk youth live in so-called at-risk communities and attend so-called failing schools. You have to take a community-wide and citywide view if you want to make an impact. Some of that passion was fueled by the growing Christian community development network that Perkins had started and some came from my involvement with Fuller, Bill Pannell, and World Vision.

I'd learned so much in my studies and from my mentors, particularly Bill, John Perkins, and Verley. Jim Wallis, one of those lonely, white evangelical voices who, early on, spoke passionately and eloquently about justice, racial reconciliation, and holistic ministry, guest lectured at Fuller. He stirred my heart when he talked about God's love for the poor and preferential attitude toward the marginalized. After reading Ron Sider's book, *Rich Christians in an Age of Hunger,* I had serious questions about America's love affair with materialism. I studied Liberation Theology with visiting professor Orlando Costas and began to understand how many Latino theologians looked at the scripture from the "underside." I read his book, *Christ Outside the Gate* and many other books that helped shape a very different worldview and gave me a theological perspective that was alien to the one bequeathed me by my upbringing.

An "Un-American" Jesus?

Ron Sider has a way of ruffling feathers, even mine. He says, "We are far more interested in whether the economy grows than in whether the lot of the poor improves. We insist on more and more, and reason that if Jesus was so un-American that he considered riches dangerous, then we must ignore or reinterpret his message."[28]

At Verley's suggestion, I called Bill Winston, the man who had told me in Pittsburgh that the inner city didn't need any more "white guys coming in on a white horse to save the ghetto kids." Bill and I had become friends since then. He was still with Young Life Urban, but also closely associated with Reid Carpenter and a holistic ministry he'd begun called the Pittsburgh Leadership Foundation. PLF's ambitious mission was to make their city as famous for Jesus Christ as it was for

---

28 Ronald J. Sider, *Rich Christians in an Age of Hunger: Moving From Affluence to Generosity* (Nashville: Thomas Nelson, 2005), 93.

steel. I visited Pittsburgh and spent the day with Reid and the PLF staff. It was as if I was seeing my own future. This was *it*. PLF was about inspiring, equipping, and resourcing indigenous leaders in the heart of Pittsburgh to do ministry at the community, grassroots level, with the singular goal of expanding God's kingdom in that city.

The next time I visited Pittsburgh, I discovered that Bill Starr, former president of Young Life, had plans to begin a similar leadership foundation in Phoenix. I had to travel there from time to time for my job with Young Life, so I thought, why not get to know Bill Starr and learn all about the start-up of this kind of ministry firsthand? Like a moth to flame, I was drawn to these guys and the work they were doing in Pittsburgh and Phoenix, so I stayed in close contact with them, gleaning as much wisdom as I could.

By the time Craig Strickland ended up hearing my musings over our kitchen table at the many dinners we shared together, I had already told Becky we needed to replicate Bill and Reid's work in Southern California. I was restless, but I was beginning to have some direction. One night, after I'd spent some time recounting the many reasons beginning a city leadership ministry was the right choice to make, Craig asked, "Why don't you do it in Memphis?"

He went on to observe something I, the so-called "visionary," had not seen. Becky was ready to get closer to home. She had loved our time in California, but it was time for this phase of the adventure to be over. It was time for a chapter change. She wanted to be closer to our parents, primarily for our children's sake. I'm sure Becky had shared this with me, but I wasn't listening. Craig was.

He then made a bold offer. If we would come back to start the Memphis Leadership Foundation, he would work to get a board together and get us funded for the first year. He didn't have a plan, but I knew that if he said he'd do it he would work tirelessly to get it done. After meeting with urban ministry leaders, pastors, and potential board members, after getting a little taste of how it was done in other cities—and a conviction that it *could*, indeed, be done—we decided that we ought to move ahead with creating the Memphis Leadership Foundation.

In the fall of 1986 and spring of 1987, we recruited board members and met with various pastors and nonprofit urban leaders to share the vision, defining a leadership foundation and how it would work. Meanwhile, I took what became my most important course in the Doctor of Ministry program: Strategic Planning. What I heard in that class from Walt Wright's lectures and from the guest speakers he brought in, readings from experts in nonprofits and business like Peter Drucker and Max De Pree, helped me shape the essential groundwork for the Memphis Leadership Foundation.

As we talked with people in Memphis, we soon discovered that a citywide ministry that would equip, resource, and encourage indigenous leaders was an odd concept for most people, a little more difficult to articulate than, say, a ministry for the homeless or a prison ministry. A local leadership foundation is not operational in that way. Our goal was to seek out the urban leaders who were already doing the work and come alongside them, equip, resource, and encourage them, helping them and their ministries grow to scale. Or, when a need arose in the city that needed tending to, we would rally people, resources, and vision to meet that need. We would be a catalyst. Most of the people we met with in Memphis, once they understood what we were about, were receptive and supportive. It wasn't until later that we discovered that a few of them were a bit apprehensive. One urban leader in particular thought that this concept would create competition for resources, unfortunately a concept we need to eradicate. We are about building the kingdom regardless of the cause God has called us to, so collaboration is key. But the dream was just the opposite. If anything, we would give urban ministry a much greater visibility than ever before. If things went as planned, all urban ministry boats would rise with the foundation's work and influence. In fact, that's exactly what happened.

Colleagues Along the Way

I met with Dr. Scott Morris who had just come to Memphis to start what is now a national model for health care, the Church Health Center. He did not know me, but he graciously agreed to a meeting. I was impressed with him right away. Here was a medical doctor and an ordained Methodist minister who had the audacity to believe that health care for the working poor was a justice mandate of the church. His focus was to provide health care for the working poor — men and women who had jobs but no health benefits. He was still in the process of recruiting volunteer doctors and health professionals from the various churches and synagogues. As I shared the vision with him, I felt a vague barrier between us, just a touch of standoffishness.

After thirty minutes or so he made a comment that helped me understand his reserve: "I haven't met many Evangelicals who really cared for the poor and the city." There's that label again, creating confusion and division. Scott would not perhaps have identified himself as an "Evangelical," though what he was doing was at the heart of the gospel and as Christ-centered as anything I had seen others do who wore the Evangelical badge. I found a colleague that day. We are not colleagues because we share the same label, but because we share the same purpose and worship the same Lord.

In the meantime, Craig Strickland met with other men and women in Memphis to gauge their interest in throwing in with us. He enlisted folks and asked them to help him raise the dollars and get some board members together to start the leadership foundation.

The people we recruited were not wealthy. They certainly couldn't bankroll the foundation. But they committed to do everything they could to make this thing work. We can never repay them for what they did for our city. I guess if I say the leadership foundation in Memphis grew from humble beginnings, this is what I mean. It was truly a humbling experience to receive this kind of capital, both in finances and friendship. In addition to these friends, World Vision U.S. Ministries got on board and supported the idea of a leadership foundation in Memphis. They gave us a $10,000 start-up grant, along with Tom Jones as a consultant. Tom and I met with a number of pastors, urban and suburban, black and white, and urban nonprofit CEOs, most of whom I knew personally.

Tom Jones was an invaluable strategist. He kept pushing us to define exactly what our mission would be. What would we do? What was our unique contribution to the Kingdom of God in Memphis? He was relentless. I learned from this experience as well as from my time in Walt Wright's class at Fuller that the mission is the main thing. It is the driving force. You must know why you exist and why that is important. You need to identify your cause and do it biblically. Our cause was to seek the shalom of the city. The way we would "operationalize" the cause was to empower indigenous leaders and others who were engaged in the cause. Tom and I worked on defining our mission during my visits to Memphis. Finally, I returned to California and began to plan in earnest our next phase of ministry. I officially resigned from Young Life in 1987, after twelve years of fruitful work and after learning the value of incarnational witness. My Young Life experience was invaluable for the next chapter in ministry.

Before we moved, we assembled a more complete board

of directors for the fledgling ministry. We incorporated in 1986 and Becky, the girls, and I got settled in Memphis in the summer of 1987 with the grant from World Vision and my Young Life retirement fund. We were off and running. But what exactly was this endeavor Becky and I and so many others were risking our time and futures and money to do? I'm glad you asked.

Whatcha gonna do?

1. What labels do you, as a follower of Christ, wear? Which of these labels could be a problem for others in your interaction with them? Do they create unnecessary barriers or open up dialogue?
2. What do you think of the notion that currently Evangelicals are known more for what they are against than what they are for?
3. How do your relationships transcend the labels?
4. Are you restless for change? Is it discontentment or perhaps a nudge from God to step out in faith? What might that step look like?

Chapter 10
The City as Playground

Cities are never random. No matter how chaotic they might seem, everything about them grows out of a need to solve a problem. In fact, a city is nothing more than a solution to a problem, that in turn creates more problems that need more solutions, until towers rise, roads widen, bridges are built, and millions of people are caught up in a mad race to feed the problem-solving, problem-creating frenzy.

—Neal Shusterman, in Downsiders

We need an urban theology

—Ray Bakke

I'll stay in Memphis

—Elvis

My Southern upbringing taught me enough about etiquette to keep me from embarrassing Becky in social situations. I'm not sure how many of the little "rules" I learned as a boy matter all that much, but some of them make sense. Others are inviolable. Like this one: never show up early to a party. You'll just be in the way, you'll stress out your host, and you'll probably feel really awkward.

But sometimes it's worth doing. John Perkins, Bill Pannell, Verley Sangster, Jim Wallis, Ron Sider, Tom Skinner and others showed up early to the party that is now in full swing in the city. And they dragged a lot of young men and women along with them. I can never thank them enough for doing so. When we set our sights on the city years ago, it was a place people couldn't exit fast enough. There was no "cool" involved in living or working in the city. Consequently, the party was small, but what a party it was.

A Theology of the City

You know how it feels when you read a book that rings true, so much so that you say to yourself, "that is exactly how I would have said it, if only I'd had the words." That's how I responded to Ray Bakke's books on city ministry. Bakke helped a lot of us formulate a theology of the city parallel to the beginning of the Memphis Leadership Foundation. As the unofficial theologian for the Leadership Foundation movement, he helped define what it was we were about to do, to give it theological roots. But he also gave us some basic biblical parameters based on his own work as a pastor. According to Ray, "If we penetrate the cities, the gospel will travel."[29] A local leadership foundation is committed to taking the whole gospel to the whole city, seeking the shalom of the city. He says, "Christians are the only people who can truly discuss the salvation of souls and the rebuilding of city sewer systems in the same sentence."[30] With this sort of theological paradigm, there is no defining line between the gospel of salvation and the social gospel. Where better for the two to fuse than in the melting pots of our cities?

---

29 Ray Bakke, *A Theology As Big As the City*, 168.

30 IBID, 34.

Bakke says, "If the Bible teaches that cities are important beyond the fact that they are collections of individuals, then our ministry in cities must be both public and private, both personal and corporate."[31] Just how important are cities in the Bible? One doesn't have to look far to find out.

Jeremiah wrote to the exiles who lived in Babylon and told them to "Build houses and settle down. Plant gardens and eat what they produce. Marry and have sons and daughters; find wives for your sons and give your daughters in marriage, so that they, too, may have sons and daughters. Increase in number there; do not decrease. Also, seek the peace and prosperity of the city to which I have carried you into exile. Pray to the Lord for it, because if it prospers, you, too, will prosper." (Jeremiah 29:5-7, NIV) Or, to use the recognizable Hebrew word, they were instructed to pray for the *shalom* of the city. Before Jeremiah, Jonah went to Nineveh, a city of "more than a hundred and twenty thousand people who cannot tell their right hand from their left." (Jonah 4:11, ESV) This was perhaps a reference to the number of innocent children who would have perished had not God relented in his anger against the city. Like Babylon, Nineveh was Israel's enemy. Nineveh was in Assyria, the ruling power that defeated the northern kingdom of Israel. And yet God asked Jonah, "Should I not be concerned about that great city?" (4:11) Clearly, cities, godless, erring, sinful cities, matter to God. And what city is more representative of God's judgment and anger than Sodom? Abraham's dialogue with the Lord about Lot and the impending destruction of Sodom and Gomorrah shows us his bent toward mercy. Abraham, thinking of his nephew Lot, asked if the city could be spared if there were fifty righteous people living in it. And God said, "If I find fifty righteous people in the city of Sodom, I will spare the

31 Bakke, *A Theology As Big As the City*, 64.

whole place for their sake." (Genesis 18:26, NIV) Abraham whittled the number of "righteous people" who might or might not live in Sodom to ten, and the Lord's answer was the same every time. This conversation reminds us that God is ever leaning toward the restoration of cities, even up until the very end when it is too late.

The destruction of Sodom happened only after the people who could have—but didn't—make a difference there had escaped. The New Testament tells us Lot was a righteous man, but I can't help but wonder if he didn't get it wrong in Sodom. The covenant God made with Abraham in Genesis 12 carries the seed of the gospel: "I will make you into a great nation and I will bless you; I will make your name great, and you will be a blessing." (Genesis 12:2, NIV) Maybe Lot didn't get the "you will be a blessing" memo. Jesus expanded this idea in the New Covenant when he told us to be salt and light in the world, a world that today is primarily urban. We are meant to flavor cities, to preserve them, to illuminate them. The presence of God's people ought to preserve places like the cities we live in with a church on every corner.

The world is now an urban or global city, no longer a global village. Over half of the world's population now live in cities. This is in stark contrast to the 20 percent who lived in cities 100 years ago. And this trend isn't changing anytime soon. Every year, the number of urban residents grows by sixty million.[32] The mission field of the twenty-first century is the city. God is bringing the nations to the cities. It has been his plan for millennia.

---

32 http://www.who.int/gho/urban_health/situation_trends/urban_popu-lation_growth_text/en/index.html

A Theology of Place

The idea that there is a correlation between the presence of God's people and the preservation of places[33] has become central to missiology for the Leadership Foundation movement. Missionaries have always known this. As God's chosen people, do we understand that we are in this or that city for his purposes and not our own? I am here for a purpose and you are in this city or in Detroit for a purpose, too. It is bigger than us. God didn't save us so that we could pursue our own agenda, our own comfort, so we could look out for ourselves alone. No, He saved us for a mission...his mission. We don't live for ourselves. We live for him and he puts us in "places" to carry out his mission.

God redeems persons within the context of place. The heroes of the Old and New Testament were often identified by the place in which they lived or from which they came. It was the same in the early church...they were known by their locations. The church at Corinth or the church at Philippi and the other churches mentioned in Paul's letters and in Revelation. I am committed to Memphis. God has something in mind for Memphis because he is Lord of this city. So many people move from city to city to pursue this or that job or career. Way too many people move because they sense that this or that city will be a better place to raise their family.

Many people have applauded me on my "success" in Memphis. But, I've simply tried to be faithful to this city over the long haul. New programs come and go. A young gun comes in to "save the city" and is gone in a couple of years or less. Just recently, in fact, a ministry that was begun by some young leaders in Memphis has decided to relocate to another southern city. They raised a lot of money in Memphis and a lot of expectations. Now they're gone.

---

33 *The Urban Christian* by Ray Bakke , p, 64, InterVarsity Press, 1987, Downers Grove

We need people committed to a theology of place. There's something to be said about a long-term commitment. Over the years I've met with dozens of young men and women who are passionate about urban ministry. They inevitably ask me how long it will take to see fruit. My standard answer has been three to five years. It takes that long to gain credibility. Frankly, I haven't seen a huge differential between black, Latino, or white urban leadership in this. I used to think that an African American leader working in an African American community would gain credibility faster than a white ministry leader. There's definitely some truth to that, but the primary ingredient comes down to time, commitment, and credibility. People in inner-city, distressed neighborhoods have been used, oppressed, bent for the political purposes of elected officials, and lied to. An outsider who shows up to "do good" is not exactly a welcome sight. The white folks coming in with all the answers reeks of age-old paternalism.

A theology of place puts place and relationships over programmatic iterations. It makes the city and its people the primary thing. When you commit to place you are taking the long view. You are committed for life!

If climbing to the top of one's career ladder is a priority versus God's agenda for his people, then theology of place makes little sense. We go to wherever it is that provides the fastest track, biggest salary, and most upwardly mobile opportunity. In fact, from a secular perspective, the right decision is always to pursue our career path. But when you see a place as sacred, like I do Memphis, then the place and serving him in the place becomes primary, far above career or opportunity. This theology of place idea is crucial to the Leadership Foundation movement, and I contend that it is crucial for the people of God. None of us is in our "place" by accident. And as his people, we have a job to do: to seek the shalom of the place God has placed us, to pray for it, to invest in it.

In the final analysis, our home is not any earthly city. According to the scriptures, we are exiles here. Abraham understood this:

> . . . *he was confidently looking forward to a city with eternal foundations, a city designed and built by God. It was by faith that Sarah together with Abraham was able to have a child, even though they were too old and Sarah was barren. Abraham believed that God would keep his promise. And so a whole nation came from this one man, Abraham, who was too old to have any children—a nation with so many people that, like the stars of the sky and the sand on the seashore, there is no way to count them. All these faithful ones died without receiving what God had promised them, but they saw it all from a distance and welcomed the promises of God. They agreed that they were no more than foreigners and nomads here on earth. And obviously people who talk like that are looking forward to a country they can call their own. If they had meant the country they came from, they would have found a way to go back. But they were looking for a better place, a heavenly homeland. That is why God is not ashamed to be called their God, for he has prepared a heavenly city for them.* —Hebrews 11:10-16, NLT

Like Abraham, we look forward to an eternal home, a heavenly city. But, like the Israelites living in Babylon, we have a responsibility to pray for and work toward the *shalom* of our temporal cities where we live as exiles. Nineveh was so important to God that he sent Jonah there to call her to repentance. From Genesis on, we have built cities. That's what we do, because we are made to be in community. We are "in" the world, in the city as instruments of redemption. Cities provide community, commerce, security, employment, health care, and more. Cities are a means of sharing God's common grace.

One of the nation's most exemplary models of God's common grace is in Memphis: St. Jude Hospital, an internationally acclaimed cancer research hospital for childhood cancer and disease. Kids from all over the world come here for medical care, many of them cured. By common grace, I mean the grace that God in his sovereign will bestows on all of humanity, like rain and sunshine so we can grow crops. Cities are a beautiful expression of that common grace. Cities house hospitals, museums, art, technology, educational institutions, commerce, music, all the things that lend life its beauty.

Learning to Listen

I learned from John Perkins that you had to listen to the community rather than presume to be an expert, especially if you haven't taken the time to really know what lies at the heart of its issues. I've seen so many leaders, white and black, come into a city or neighborhood with this or that program, the latest, greatest thing that they proclaim will transform the city or community. And I've seen so many of them come and go. If a community wants to be transformed, then leadership in that community will ultimately be the transforming agents. The role of the leader, particularly if the leader is not a member of the community, is to listen and come alongside those change agents, assist when possible, lead when necessary, and work with the people to change their own community.

Frankly, I've grown weary of the new guys who blow in and then blow out of the city, paternalistically declaring what's best for a particular neighborhood, only to create chaos, distrust, and often leaving behind a wake of broken promises. And they wonder why the community didn't "appreciate" what they were trying to do, in effect, placing blame for their failure on the very people they were trying to "help." We need people who will stay and see things through, people who will take the theology of place seriously. In his book, When Helping Hurts, *Brian Fikkert explores this very issue, noting that "top-down helping" can be hurtful in the short and long term.*[34]

In 1987, after six years in California, with the Pittsburgh Leadership Foundation as our model, and Verley Sangster, Fred Davis, and Bill Pannell as my mentors, I decided to commit the rest of my life to the city of Memphis. That may sound somewhat arrogant, I suppose. I mean, shouldn't believers go anywhere God sends them? Aren't we to be open to go anywhere at any time? The answer of course is a resounding "yes." But this is my way of committing myself to God's will in this city for the rest of my life. If God wants me to do something else, he will make it clear.

Back when we first formed MLF, most people either romanticized the city (think *West Side Story*) or were terrified of it (think *Requiem for a Dream*). Mention "inner-city ministry" and they imagined a lone ranger prowling the streets like David Wilkerson in *The Cross and the Switchblade*. If you defined your ministry in terms of a specific target, like the homeless or teen gang members, people got it. But a local leadership foundation's bodacious purpose is to mobilize the whole church to love the whole city and seek its peace, and that's a little harder to grasp. We never planned to accomplish this by competing with existing ministries, some of which I had already helped create like Young Life Urban and Neighborhood Christian Centers. Our goal was to come alongside those ministries and others, to help them in any way we could, to strengthen them, but also to look

---

34 Brian Fikkert, Steve Corbett, David Platt, *When Helping Hurts: How to Alleviate Poverty Without Hurting the Poor . . . and Yourself* (Chicago: Moody Publishers, 2012), 108.

for the grassroots leaders no one had yet discovered or encouraged.

Some time ago, I heard Chuck Colson speak in a Memphis home about the ministry he was then starting, Prison Fellowship. He used a "little platoon" analogy that has stuck with me ever since. Everywhere, in every city and in every community, God has his little platoons of saints who are salt and light and are impacting their neighborhoods. These people are committed to their particular place. We saw our job as a leadership foundation to engage, support, equip, and empower these platoons, and more specifically, the platoon leaders.

We decided to create an umbrella for grassroots urban leaders so they could flesh out God's call on their lives. We would provide back office support (bookkeeping, data collection, donor records), plus benefits like major medical and health insurance that they couldn't afford as a small ministry. We would also provide encouragement, strategic planning, and accountability. We would empower ministries with the management tools I had learned from Walt Wright, Peter Drucker, Max De Pree, and others while at Fuller. We would help these urban pioneers and heroes learn how to raise funds, implement programs, write grants, establish a board of directors, care for and feed their volunteers, interface with suburban and urban churches to share their vision, etc. Most of all, we would listen to their dreams and vision for their piece of the city to which God had called them, and we would do what we could to help those dreams come to fruition.

We could enjoy economies of scale that smaller ministries could benefit from. Rather than each of them hiring accountants, buying computers and all that it takes these days to manage a ministry, we could consolidate all their infrastructures at the foundation, thus empowering these urban leaders to do what they do best: reach the poor and marginalized with the gospel and expand God's kingdom in our city, but in a way that empowered the very recipients of this gospel to realize God's full potential for them. But first I had to get there.

Getting to Memphis at Last

Before we left Pasadena in 1987, I got a call from an African American Presbyterian Church in Memphis inquiring if I would serve as their interim pastor until their new pastor came in early 1988. Craig Strickland had given them my name. The "interview" was done via telephone while I was still in California. I accepted the position knowing that I wouldn't get a salary for some time. The interview was conducted with the clerk of the session (an elder in Presbyterian Church polity), Bill Jones, who would later become one of my closest colleagues.

I preached my first sermon at Parkway Gardens Presbyterian in July 1987. I arrived early that first Sunday and quickly discovered that everyone thought I would be African American. Craig had forgotten to tell them I was white, and Bill Jones didn't ask me in our interview. I assumed they knew what color I was. Six months of wonderful ministry at Parkway Gardens followed. They had accepted me with open arms. Bill Jones would later become one of the first employees at MLF as director of a brand-new job placement program funded in part by World Vision. The Black Caucus of Memphis Presbytery, of which Parkway Gardens was a key player, would also become the future impetus behind a teen pregnancy prevention program that MLF would start in collaboration with them in the months ahead.

Meanwhile, MLF was off and running. The first office was in our home in Memphis. It was definitely a faith leap. I had a wonderfully supportive wife and four daughters: Leah (nine), Lydia (seven), Charis and Hannah (five), a fledgling board of directors, an ambiguous mission with an even more ambiguous name, and extended family who were just glad we were back in Memphis.

After a few months the board decided we needed a permanent address, so we secured office space on Poplar Avenue, the main drag in Memphis. We had kept the $10,000 from World Vision intact, and we used some of that to set up the office. Our first MLF computer system was the Radio Shack TRSDOS 80 with two floppies on which I had just finished my doctoral dissertation over the summer.

Craig, along with Fred Davis, and others, assembled a board of seventeen men and women. Except for Fred and one other, the board was quite young, pretty much all in their thirties. I continued to meet with all the urban ministry leaders in the city. I met with dozens of pastors. It was all coming together. I dreamed that Memphis Leadership Foundation would become a vehicle that would solidify the "little platoons" and the "platoon leaders" who were making a huge difference in our city but for whom there was little support or resource. When possible and necessary, we would create new programs, but only in response to real need as opposed to creating a program for programs' sake. The only way to make wise decisions was to hear from the city itself. So we began to listen to our city and her urban leaders. Memphis had stories to tell and we were ready to hear them.

Whatcha gonna do?

1. How is the gospel both "public and private, both personal and corporate" in your life and ministry?
2. Do you have a "theology of place," especially as it relates to your city? If so, how would you describe it?
3. Why do you think God has you in your city? What does he want you to do in your city?
4. What are some steps you can take to listen to your city?

Chapter 11

Repentance, Justice, Righteousness, and Privilege

When Israel was in Egypt's land: Let my people go,
Oppress'd so hard they could not stand, Let my People go.
Go down, Moses,
Way down in Egypt's land,
Tell old Pharaoh,
Let my people go.

—Song of the Underground Railroad,
originally published by the Jubilee Singers in 1872.

Why reasonable people go stark raving mad when something
involving a Negro comes up is something I don't pretend to
understand. I just hope Jeb and Scout come to me for their
answers instead of listening to the town[35]

—Atticus Finch in *To Kill a Mockingbird*

Where justice is denied, where poverty is enforced, where
ignorance prevails, and where any one class is made to feel
that society is an organized conspiracy to oppress, rob and
degrade them, neither persons nor property will be safe.

—Frederick Douglass, in a 1886 speech

---

35 Harper Lee, *To Kill a Mockingbird* (New York: Harper, 50th Anniversary Edition, 2010), 145.

Quaker abolitionist Levi Coffin and his wife, Catherine, helped as many as 2,000 slaves escape to freedom. Their home in Ohio was such a strategic pit stop in the vast network of secret routes and safe houses known as the Underground Railroad that it was called Grand Central Station. That earns the Coffins a gold star in my book. But their involvement in the railroad is only part of their story. Levi Coffin's role in the abolition movement was more than a noble venture, it was a dangerous one. Not only could it have ruined him, it could have killed him as well. And it almost did. When his friends and family warned him about the perils of his chosen vocation, he wrote:

> After listening quietly to these counselors, I told them that I felt no condemnation for anything that I had ever done for the fugitive slaves. If by doing my duty and endeavoring to fulfill the injunctions of the Bible, I injured my business, then let my business go. As to my safety, my life was in the hands of my Divine Master, and I felt that I had his approval. I had no fear of the danger that seemed to threaten my life or my business. If I was faithful to duty, and honest and industrious, I felt that I would be preserved, and that I could make enough to support my family[36]

Not long after moving to Indiana from North Carolina, where he had learned to hate slavery as a young boy, he became a business owner and merchant, eventually investing in and directing a local bank. Coffin's success gave him the means to invest heavily in transportation, clothing, and food for escaping slaves. Apparently the Coffins understood the importance of relocating in order to fully incarnate the gospel. They made a very intentional move to Cincinnati, so

36 Mary Ann Yannessa, *Levi Coffin, Quaker: Breaking the Bonds of Slavery in Ohio and Indiana* (Richmond: Friends United Press, 2001), 24.

that Levi could operate a warehouse that sold goods produced by free labor. The business ultimately failed. Even so, Coffin continued to house escaping slaves. After the Thirteenth Amendment passed and slaves were emancipated, Coffin traveled the world establishing aid organizations for freed slaves.

I'd like to think I'd have been a Levi Coffin in those days. But I wonder. Would I have risked my reputation, my livelihood, perhaps even my life for people of another race? Would I have understood, as so few did then, that enslaving a fellow human being regardless of and especially because of his or her skin color was morally reprehensible? Would I have dared to act on that belief? Again, I'd like to think I'd have been like Levi Coffin, swimming upstream against the powerful current of the prevailing culture. I hope, if I'd lived a few years later, I would have been like Atticus Finch in *To Kill a Mockingbird*, a man who championed the cause of a wrongly accused black man. But, for all intents and purposes, the past is like Atticus: fiction. What matters is now. And what tells me who I would have been then is who I am now.

I have a problem with people who say, "I am not a racist" or "I don't see color." "I'm color blind." That's like saying, "I am not a sinner. I'm a good person." It doesn't ring true. The thing is, although many of us are not overtly racist, we do see color. And, because we aren't perfectly righteous, we don't always respond to the colors we see righteously. The fact is, we must not only see color, we must celebrate it. God created diversity and one of the most beautiful expressions of that diversity is in the colors of our skin. But how do we get there? How can we bury the past prejudices that keep buzzing around in the back of our minds?

Because I am white, I can only speak from that perspective. These are the hard questions I ask myself. Maybe I am not overtly racist, but am I privileged in ways that my black brothers and sisters are not? Do I benefit from my "status" as a white person? Do I benefit from the racism of the past and present? And even though in 1980 the "center of gravity had shifted [from a white majority], and now the majority of Christians in the world are non-white, non-Northern, and non-Western,"[37] do I understand, behave, and make choices based on my minority status, or do I cling to the belief that I am the majority and should, therefore, get preferential treatment? This is subtle, but sinister. Do I consider what it might be like to be followed suspiciously in the drugstore as I go from aisle to aisle selecting items to put in my cart? Have I ever, once, wondered if the police pulled me over because of my race? And, most importantly, do I care about any of this since, after all, it does not affect me?

Who Can Best Define Racism?

"At the heart of racism is the idea that a man is not a man."
Reverend James Lawson

I wonder if our culture has defined racism a little too objectively. Reverend Lawson's definition of racism is both a historical and a personal one. He describes it from the perspective of living, breathing victims of racism. According to Lawson, racism is more than a noun, more than a defective belief; it is a verb that does damage to another human being. Call racism this and it stings like a physical blow. No wonder Malcolm X — clearly using Lawson's working definition — called us "White Devils." We weren't just racists; we wielded racism as a weapon. We're not comfortable with this terminology. The vitriolic anger of the Black Man is unseemly to us. But who is most qualified to describe the point of a dagger? The one who feels its point as it is driven home, that's who.

---

37 Bakke, *A Theology As Big As the City*, 145.

Asleep in Our Privilege

Of the seven churches addressed in the book of Revelation, I wonder if the church at Laodicea is perhaps the most like the white evangelical church. The believers there had a false sense of security based upon their privilege. Jesus describes what was in their hearts this way: "You say, 'I am rich. I have everything I want. I don't need a thing!' And you don't realize that you are wretched and miserable and poor and blind and naked." (Revelation 3:17, NLT)

Privilege is like that. It lulls you to sleep until you desperately need a wake-up call, a diagnosis that shocks and dismays you enough to really hear it. I am sure Jesus's words stung the first time those to whom they were written read them. But maybe, like the church at Ephesus, his words also reminded the Laodiceans of their first love, a love that offers something better than privilege:

> I advise you to buy gold from me—gold that has been purified by fire. Then you will be rich. And also buy white garments so you will not be shamed by your nakedness. And buy ointment for your eyes so you will be able to see. I am the one who corrects and disciplines everyone I love.
> (Revelation 3:18-19a, NLT)

This chapter is not a call to activism; it is a call to repentance. A wake-up call. It's no accident that the first recorded lyrics to a Christian song tell us to "Wake up, O sleeper, rise from the dead and Christ will shine on you." (Ephesians 5:14, NIV) We gravitate to sleep and sin. But, you may say, exactly what am I repenting of? I haven't done anything specifically racist that I can think of. Others may, but "I really don't see color." But what else do you not see?

Maybe the most heinous sin of all, more insidious than

racism, is complacency. Jesus tells the Laodiceans to run as fast as they can from it. He directs the church to "be diligent and turn from your indifference." (Revelation 3:19, NLT)

So how do we repent? Do all American Christians need to quit their jobs and start an urban ministry? Do we write masses of apology letters? Do we pull our kids out of their suburban schools and put them in the urban ones? Do we sell everything we have and give it to the poor? What, pray tell, are we supposed to do?

Jesus gives an answer, and it's not all that complicated. On the heels of his warning about indifference, he says, "Look! Here I stand at the door and knock. If you hear me calling and open the door, I will come in, and we will share a meal as friends." (Revelation 3:20, NLT) This passage is not written to unbelievers, although we typically use it to share the gospel with them. It is written to complacent Christians.

The whole of scripture echoes this invitation. The prophet Hosea gave a similar solution to a similarly broken people, a people who had forgotten who they were and why they existed, whose love for God and others had vanished "like the morning mist" and disappeared "like dew in the sunlight." (Hosea 6:4, NLT) He pled with them:

> Come, let us return to the LORD! He has torn us in pieces; now he will heal us. He has injured us; now he will bandage our wounds. In just a short time, he will restore us so we can live in his presence. Oh, that we might know the LORD! Let us press on to know him! Then he will respond to us as surely as the arrival of dawn or the coming of rains in early spring. (Hosea 6:1-3, NLT)

This is the road of repentance that leads to our soul's repair. Yes, we have in our privilege refused real compassion to those who are not as privileged as we are. Yes, we have racist hearts. Our love for God and for others wanes like daylight at dusk. Yes, we're not right at our very core. Let's just admit it. But we have a Righteous Savior who calls us to himself.

Affirmative action may be a good thing in certain circumstances, but it will not cure the human soul of all its ills, including racism. Notice that Jesus did not say, "If you hear me calling, go run out and start a ministry." Hosea did not say, "Come, let us return to a flurry of activity." As Oswald Chambers says, "The questions that matter in life are remarkably few, and they are all answered by the words, 'Come unto Me.'"

I Am

Often the focus of repentance is on the sin from which we repent, but I'd like to focus more on the God to whom we return. The God Hosea urged us to "press on to know." What is he like?

Some of God's attributes are transcendent, which means we could never in a million years copy them. These are the qualities Eve craved in the garden. God is omniscient, omnipresent, and omnipotent. All-knowing, all-present, and all-powerful. We, on the other hand, are born deluded about ourselves. We think we know more than we do. We think we can fill our schedules, trick time, and be in more than one place at once. And we think we can control far more than we really can, leading to an inflated sense of power. It takes years for us to conclude that it is best to let God be God in these areas.

When he met Moses at the burning bush, God said, "I am that I am." He is both self-existent, meaning he does not rely on anyone or anything for his existence, and he is self-sufficient, meaning he does not, like us, have needs that must be

met by anyone but himself. He is eternal. All of these qualities make him distinctly "other than" us. They are more than
adequate fodder for worship. The angels recognized God's
transcendent character, and when they sing to him, they
always affirm that he is worthy of their praise. No human
being is worthy in the same way.

God's transcendence is important to know and understand. The more we grasp it—and we never can, fully—the
more we live in holy awe of who he is. But God is not only
transcendent, he is a God who wants his kingdom subjects to
look like him. He wants his children to bear his resemblance.
This is not only his desire, it is his pre-engineered plan. He
made us to mirror him.

So now understanding him becomes even more essential.
How can we look like a God we do not know? We are stamped
with the *Imago Dei*, the image of God, but that image has been
disfigured by our sin. If we'll return to him and learn from
him, the image will form more accurately, more beautifully.

Justice and Righteousness

There are two aspects of his character I'm afraid my generation has missed or misunderstood, and I'd like to highlight
them here because as we understand and embrace these
aspects in our lives, we can begin to be the ambassadors of
his reconciliation more ably.

In the Hebrew texts of the Old Testament, justice and righteousness often appear together. In fact, the two words are
often fused into one as a *hendiadys*, a Greek and Latin figure
of speech in which two words connected by a conjunction
are used to express a single complex idea. The two words are
mishpat, or justice, and *sedeq*, righteousness. There are over
fifty instances of these two ideas tied together in a *hendiadys*
in the Old Testament. For example, in Amos 5:24: "But let

justice roll down like waters, and righteousness like an ever-flowing stream."

This *hendiadys* which includes references to trampling upon the poor and turning aside the needy makes it clear that God is concerned about justice and righteousness. That is, God is concerned about personal holiness or sanctification in our lives, what we might refer to as righteousness, and he is equally concerned about social justice. The prophets did not see any distinction between spiritual bankruptcy and the social bankruptcy that reflects it. In Psalm 33:5 we are told that, "God loves righteousness and justice." In Proverbs 21:3, we are reminded that "to do righteousness and justice is more acceptable to the Lord than sacrifice."

Salvation language in the Old Testament has a strong social and this-worldly flavor in contrast to an individualistic understanding of salvation that many of us have today. In Isaiah 1:16 there is a seamless progression of thought: "Wash yourselves, make yourselves clean," which refers to obedience to the commandments, followed by, "seek justice, correct oppression; defend the fatherless, plead for the widow." Clearly, personal rightness and public "rightness" go hand in hand.

Every nation, whether capitalist, socialist, or communist, has laws and regulations that are supposed to make that society just. Again, no society can do this correctly, and even in the best of systems justice is biased. For example, in America, laws meant to create justice only did so for white America prior to the civil rights era.

God instituted the Jubilee Year in order to judicially enforce social justice in the kingdom of Israel.[38] Every fifty years, all land was to revert back to the original owners without compensation. Almost every Jew understood that the land they "owned" was actually the Lord's. Men were merely his

---

38 Leviticus 24

stewards. The Jubilee year began, significantly, on the Day of Atonement when the sins of the people were forgiven. The connection between personal righteousness and social justice is impossible to dismiss.

Moses, taught by the Lord, understood that sinful people create sinful societies and cultures. We will always produce poor people. We will allow injustice to trump justice if given the least chance. However, rather than throwing up his hands and declaring the equivalent of "boys will be boys," Yahweh ordered his people to create legislation that promoted justice. Like an artisan applying constant pressure to a pot on a wheel, God continually shapes his people, individually and collectively, into his image.

We have no record in the Bible that the Jubilee Year was ever practiced in Israel. Disobedience, however, does not negate God's demand for justice. In fact, much of the prophetic denunciation against Israel was about injustice toward the poor, the orphan, the widow, and the stranger. Had Israel obeyed the Lord on this issue, is it possible that there would have been no poor among them? That was certainly God's intention for them, so it's hard not to wonder how it would have turned out if Israel had obeyed. "But there will be no poor among you; for the LORD will bless you in the land that the LORD your God is giving you for an inheritance to possess." (Deuteronomy 15:4, ESV)

One way to define righteousness, *sedeqah*, is being right, doing the right thing, that which God deems right, and living in right relationship with God. And justice, *misphat*, means doing right things toward others, treating people according to God's will and moral law, according to God's mercy, and more pointedly, acting justly toward and on behalf of those who are treated unjustly. The two are really synonymous. That is to say, my vertical relationship with the Lord is tied into my horizontal relationships in the world. If justice and righteousness were indispensable to God's kingdom, Israel, in the Old Testament, then surely these attributes are present in the messianic kingdom that Jesus came to inaugurate. Many modern day Evangelicals act as if the primary teaching of Jesus relates only to personal salvation. But most biblical scholars would agree that the primary theme of Jesus's teaching and preaching was not only about individual salvation, but the collective "Kingdom of God." Jesus's message resounded with the truth that "The Kingdom of God is at Hand." Personal salvation is certainly one aspect of this kingdom, but if it is the only aspect we give any credence to, I submit that we are not thinking biblically. We are thinking more like children, really. Children see the world only as it impacts them. The essence of their innocence is self-absorption. Indeed, one message of the kingdom is that we can be made right personally before a holy God because of the sacrifice he made on the cross that atoned for our sins. We can, like Hosea instructs, come to him. In fact, this is the "gateway" truth that initiates us into the kingdom. Each and every one of us starts out in the kingdom as a self-centered child. "We love because he first loved us" is a statement that reminds us of these humble beginnings.

But we dare not stop there. Hosea also told us to "press on to know the Lord," which means knowing his full character and assimilating it into our own lives. He is the God who "saw" Hagar in the wilderness when his own servants, Abraham and Sarah, had closed their eyes to her and her plight.[39] He is, according to Isaiah, a compassionate God who feels with those who suffer.[40] His kingdom is about social righteousness as much as it is about personal righteousness. For years, conservative Evangelicalism has divorced personal discipleship from social justice. This is why the majority of

---

39 In Genesis 16:13, Hagar calls the Lord "The God of seeing."

40 Isaiah 54:7-8

white Christians in both the South and the North defended slavery, segregation, and Jim Crow. This is how our leaders could justify statements like Jefferson Davis's, that slavery was "established by decree of Almighty God...it is sanctioned in the Bible, in both Testaments, from Genesis to Revelation... it has existed in all ages, has been found among the people of the highest civilization, and in nations of the highest proficiency in the arts."[41]

This is why we sat idly by and watched African American Christians fight for civil rights while white conservative Christians smugly called it liberal theology. This is why whites moved to the suburbs when fair housing laws were passed, and put their kids in private schools or suburban schools when school desegregation began.

"I Stand at the Door and Knock"

A personal relationship with Christ, one in which we are made righteous before a holy God, is a privilege. I don't want to make light of this. That he stands at the door of our hearts and asks admittance there is the biggest honor humankind has ever known. And that he would enter and sit at the table of our lives and dine with us, well, I find that overwhelming. It is beyond mercy. But if I may be so bold, I'd like to add one more image to this knock-at-the-door metaphor, one that I think reflects the just and loving nature of God:

The table groans under the weight of the bounty God provides. He sits at the head of the table and we sit nearby, drinking in his presence. As we discover more about the God who is both guest and host in the dining room of our hearts, we begin to think and act as he would. We go with him to knock on others' doors. We invite them to join us at the table. We may "see color," but the differences in others only give us

41 http://www.newworldencyclopedia.org/entry/Abolitionism

greater cause to embrace them and welcome them in. "Come in," we say, "Our Master is holding a feast."

And then, when we are satisfied that the chairs are full and no one is slighted or left out or refused or wounded or cheated, only then, we ask a blessing and dig in.

Whatcha gonna do?

1. If you are white, how have you benefited from white privilege? If you are black, how has white privilege created a disadvantage for you?
2. In either case, how have you been complacent toward those in need in your city?
3. What steps must you take to repent?

Chapter 12

The Wheels on the Bus

*There are risks and costs to action. But they are far less than
the long range risks of comfortable inaction.*

—John F. Kennedy

*Empowering urban men, women, boys, and girls through
creative ministry and effective leadership.*

—Mission Statement of the Memphis Leadership Foundation

Since 1987, we've put "wheels on the bus." We've developed concrete avenues towards seeking the "shalom" of our city. Below are some examples of how we've loved our city.

- Over 300 homes built and sold/rented at a value of $21 million through Neighborhood Housing Opportunities.
- Fifteen hundred men and women have been placed in sustainable jobs through Memphis Jobs, Economic Opportunities, and Memphis Economic Development Partnership.
- Seven fully equipped primary health care medical clinics and one mobile unit provide spiritual and medical care to those in need through Christ

149

Community Health Services. Over 65,000 patients are served each year, most with limited or no health insurance.

- Two thousand juvenile offense cases have been mediated, reducing recidivism from 38 percent to less than 10 percent for juvenile offenders through Mediation and Restitution/Reconciliation Services.
- Ten thousand urban youth are served through a variety of youth outreach ministries all over the city.
- Over 7,500 inner city youth attend For the Kingdom Camp for one week.
- Three hundred fifty immigrant and refugee youth participate in reading and tutoring programs through MultiNational Ministries and the Refugee Empowerment Program.
- Over 180 youth workers have been trained and over 10,000 youth are involved regularly through the Urban Youth Initiative Program.
- Numerous recreation and athletic facilities have been established with thousands of kids served each year through Memphis Athletic Ministries.
- Memphis Center for Urban Theological Studies (MCUTS): a collaboration between MLF, Second Presbyterian Church, Hope Christian Community Foundation, Neighborhood Christian Centers and Hope Presbyterian Church, MCUTS targets urban pastors and ministry leaders with undergraduate degrees in biblical studies with the aim to empower inner city grass roots churches to be transformers of their neighborhoods. Over 150 pastors and urban ministry leaders are being empowered. Additionally, post graduate programs are offered as well.

We aren't parading these numbers before you to impress you, but because without them there's not much evidence of our commitment. What's listed above is the partial outcome of what's been said in the preceding chapters about racism and privilege, about righteousness and justice, about leadership and grassroots ministry empowerment...about seeking the peace of our city. What good are biblical values, noble callings, or good ideas unless we act on them? What good is a shiny new bus without its wheels? It may appear useful and sound like it can get the job done when the motor runs, but it will end up in the rust heap with weeds caressing its undercarriage if it doesn't do what it was meant to do: move forward. I want to tell some success stories that illustrate how we got the wheels rolling in our city.

STREETS

Ken Bennett is the executive director of STREETS, an inner-city youth outreach ministry that is arguably one of the best models for sustainable youth ministry in the nation. Ken had volunteered with us in Orange Mound with Young Life Urban when he was just out of college. When we met again, he was working in the Foote and Cleaborn Homes Housing Project area with a Catholic parish. Foote and Cleaborn Homes are two of Memphis's older public housing communities, and at one time located in one of the poorest zip codes in the nation. This massive federally subsidized apartment community was home to thousands of people, pretty much all of them living below the poverty line. Many notable African American leaders started out there, just south of downtown Memphis. Some of the surrounding federal housing projects have been torn down and replaced with the Hope VI program of the Federal Department of Housing and Urban Development (HUD).

Public housing is a vivid example of institutional sin. Some would be kinder and call the resulting generational poverty an unintended consequence. But whether unintentional or not, the result was the same and could have been forecast. Many African American families living at poverty levels were relegated to this one zip code where everyone was poor. The results of this tactic have been devastating. There are few men in the projects because AFDC (Aid to Families with Dependent Children) was only available to single-parent families. This policy, wittingly or unwittingly, worked against intact families. The erosion of family and culture continues today. Public housing policy, intended to be short term, provided decent housing when built, but by the 1970s and '80s, provided substandard housing at best and deplorable conditions at worst, in some cases. By the 1980s, most of the public housing stock had already outlived its expected lifespan. Work was dis-incentivized over time because benefits were reduced as income expanded. Nuclear families were discouraged because policies favored single-parent homes. And the result: a "ghetto" of people locked in poverty and locked out of the mainstream economy. It doesn't take but one or two generations of being subjected to this system to create a "welfare generation" among a people group. And public housing is just one of many examples of how injustice, racism, and sin can become "institutionalized" within a culture or bureaucratic policy. And, of course, the poor are blamed in the end!

God had placed on Ken's heart a real burden and passion for the young people in this community, kids for whom few positive role models existed. Kids who seldom saw a father get up early and go to work, come home with a paycheck, and put bread on the table would have a hard time understanding the work world in later years. Unemployment was the rule, and gainful employment the exception. Ken was a humble, almost shy, skinny guy. There was nothing flashy about him, but he was faithful and he knew what God had called him to do. Anyone who knew Ken knew that if he was your friend, you could count on him.

We had lunch one day at a favorite restaurant in Memphis, the Buntyn Café, which was famous for its homemade yeast rolls, cornbread, and fried chicken. He told me of his burden for kids and asked if we could help him get his ministry idea up and running. This is exactly what we had envisioned MLF doing: coming alongside a bona fide urban ministry leader who had a vision, passion and idea but who was short on money, infrastructure, and board members.

So we decided to help Ken put wheels on his vision. For starters, Ken had an old van. We hadn't raised much money yet, but the board was all over this and we had a "banquet" coming up and the $10,000 from World Vision. We had no idea how we were going to pay Ken a salary, but we stacked our hands together and worked hard to help him raise more funds down the road.

We spent a lot of time planning for the STREETS ministry, and we launched it in the fall of 1987. The name STREETS stuck, because without a building and just the van, Ken literally was meeting kids on the streets, at school, and at the hangout places. Ken and I were the first official MLF staffers, and our bookkeeper was board member Becky Maddux. She, Craig Strickland, and others were our first champions and helped us to get the whole thing started. We held the banquet in October, raised over $40,000, and the rest, as they say, is history. The board worked hard and God blessed us with the resources we needed to get the job done. Sure, it wasn't easy. There was the stock market "crash" in 1987, followed by more tough times, but God was and is faithful. He has provided for the ministry from day one until today.

Ken did what all effective urban youth workers do. He

"incarnated" the gospel, meaning he was in the community all the time. He was a fixture at local Booker T. Washington High School and later at Vance Middle School. He partnered with local churches and established credibility with the pastors in the community. His wife Debbie was as committed to the ministry as he was, and together they forged a great ministry that has seen immeasurable fruit. And it all started with $10,000 and a beat-up van.

Memphis Jobs

As soon as we started planning for STREETS, we became aware of another unmet need in our city. Unemployment was high in 1987. Through my networking in the city I increasingly encountered men and women, particularly men, who were unemployed or underemployed but who had job skills and a drive to work. They just couldn't get in the door. During this time, World Vision U.S. Ministries started a national jobs program that focused on this same population: men and women who were employable but locked out for various reasons. One reason might have been a run-in with the law and a resulting criminal record. Another reason might be minimal education, inability to interview well, or even a lack of reading ability. I asked Bill Jones, the clerk of the session of the church I was serving, if he would consider heading up what we would eventually call "Memphis Jobs," and he agreed. We got a second grant from World Vision and started in the fall of 1987, about the same time we were getting STREETS off the ground. Within one year, MLF had incubated two ministries.

Bill is a Memphian who had raised his family and was ready to tackle this ministry head-on. He did so with quiet passion. Bill is the consummate gentleman, an incredible example to me and others of quiet determination. The Memphis Jobs ministry was well laid out by World Vision. We simply put our own Memphis touch on it. It was immediately successful in its mission to come alongside men and women who, because of insurmountable barriers, were unable to get a living-wage job. An economic impact study for the Memphis Jobs ministry indicated that millions of dollars in wages for men and women who had previously been unemployed or underemployed had been leveraged, not to mention the fact that the same families no longer had to depend on food stamps or public housing. Eventually, Memphis Jobs would expand to meet another need through a ministry created in the early 1990s called Economic Opportunities.

There were some men we couldn't empower through Memphis Jobs. No one would hire men with criminal records who had served prison time. So we created Economic Opportunities to address this need in our city, actually creating a small business ourselves where we could train these men, do twelve-step programs, lead devotionals, work on financial literacy, and give them a job history. This venture, too, was hugely successful.

Measuring the Results

One of our MLF objectives was to empower leaders in their ministries. Another was to provide the back-office support, benefits, and other services in a cost-effective way. Phoebe Hover came on the staff in early 1988 to be our bookkeeper, administrator, and "jack-of-all-trades." I'm convinced that Phoebe can walk on water, though I've never seen her do it firsthand. Phoebe did the books for all the ministries, kept donor records and receipts, and managed much of the business side of MLF, allowing Ken, Bill, and others to concentrate on ministry. Phoebe enabled us to do the work of MLF as we'd dreamed we would do it.

Another objective was not only to empower ministry leaders through operational support, but also to help them develop their leadership skills. They were encouraged to put together a "board of advisors" for their ministries. They were trained in fund-raising, how to read a balance sheet, and other necessary administrative skills should they at some point want their independence and come out from under the MLF umbrella. Our purpose was to empower, encourage, and even incubate ministries. We weren't necessarily interested in keeping ministries, but we never kicked any ministry out. For the most part, this decision was ultimately the leader's to make.

As MLF began to grow exponentially and more and more ministry leaders were empowered to create new programs, the board suggested we increase our administrative staff by one. At the time, I was the "president" and Phoebe was effectively the CFO/COO. That was it. What we needed was a vice president of field ministries, someone who could continue empowering the leaders under our umbrella and create better accountability and data collection so we could effectively measure our results.

The idea of measuring results is now commonplace in nonprofit management. Most ministry types hate this sort of thing. "If just one person comes to faith, then it's all worth it," I would often hear. And, while from an eternal perspective this may be true, donors, government agencies, and foundation officials want to see results. I'll never forget when the importance of measurement first hit me. I was at a missions conference at the church where I grew up. This same church, First Evangelical, provided the second grant we needed to launch Neighborhood Christian Centers back in 1977-78. I sat with my father as a young lady gave a missionary report that went something like this: "For the last two years I've been in school in this Third World country, learning the language. Thank you for your support." My dad leaned over to me and said, "We've supported her for two years now to learn the language? She hasn't done any ministry at all? This is a waste of resources." My dad is a gracious and generous man and has always contributed to mission work in Memphis and throughout the world. We hosted missionaries in our house every missions conference. What he was really saying was this: "What are your results? Have you led anyone to faith? Have you built any wells to get clean drinking water to the people? Has anyone been helped in the name of Christ?"

From the beginning, MLF has been keen on measuring results. We were told by any number of leaders that we shouldn't be so intent on this, but the day was coming when good intentions would not be enough. If you don't measure results, how do you know what you're accomplishing?

We needed someone who could tend to our ongoing programs. This would then allow me to spend more time on the business, creativity, and fund-raising side of the ministry. The board was growing and maturing. There were more opportunities than we could shake a stick at. I suppose many would call me a ministry "entrepreneur," which is an apt description. I like to work alongside leaders to clarify their vision, create a strategy, and begin the implementation. What I don't do so well is ongoing management after a ministry or program hits stride. I'm ready to see what God is up to next, ready to move on to the next thing.

We needed a right-hand person who would help the ministries not only stabilize but grow to the proverbial "next level." The board agreed and we started a search. We had a number of applicants, but Howard Eddings rose to the top. Howard was a Memphian who had grown up in Orange Mound. I first met Howard in "the Mound" when I was working with Young Life. He had come to faith in that ministry, finished college, and was the Young Life Urban director when we asked him to become the vice president of MLF.

Howard started with MLF in 1991 as vice president, and we really began to get traction with him on board. Several other ministry leaders came on, too, and new ministries were created including Multi-National Ministries, Neighborhood Housing Opportunities, Neighborhood Housing Opportunities Management, Christ Community Health Services, Urban Youth Initiative, Memphis Athletic Ministries, Memphis Center for Urban Theological Studies, and others.[42]

Howard and a subcommittee developed a procedure whereby we could determine whether a ministry was ready to "launch" out on their own if they chose to. Everything at MLF is about empowerment at one level or another. A five-year plan was developed for each ministry that, if followed, would create independence for that ministry. The idea was to empower the leadership so that they did not need us anymore. This would free up resources for the next fledgling ministry or new venture. In the process, however, we also discovered that we could assist ministries in their start-up phase without their ever being officially a part of MLF.

Christ Community Health Services

Four young doctors met in medical school and were burdened by the Lord with the same thing: to serve the poor in the city by creating a medical practice in the heart of the most medically underserved communities. One of these young doctors did his residency at the MED, Memphis's "charity" hospital. He called his three friends and persuaded them that Memphis was the place to live out their passion. At the

---

42 You can learn more about these ministries by visiting the MLF website: www.memphisleadershipfoundation.org

time, I didn't know Rick, Steve, Karen, or David. I got a call from one of the pastors at a local church who told me about their dream and asked if I would meet with them. The pastor loved what they wanted to accomplish but just didn't know how to help them. The church had never done anything like this. We met for lunch at a barbecue joint downtown, and I was impressed with this group right away. We found some money from one of our donors, seeded their vision with a loan, helped with the strategy, and I became the board chairman. The ministry was never officially "owned" by MLF. We simply handled their finances at the beginning as their "fiscal agent" until they received all the necessary documentation from the state and federal government. Christ Community Health Services almost didn't survive a rocky start, but today it is one of the nation's largest Christ-centered medical ministries, with seven neighborhood clinics and a mobile medical van ministry for refugees and the homeless.

Again, the idea behind MLF was working: come alongside the people whom God had raised up and simply help and encourage them to accomplish his will in his city in any way we can. Each ministry requires a different strategy. MLF is creative and able to work in any number of ways, to utilize its resources very efficiently, and, in most cases, to help the leaders we work with get networked into the appropriate communities for future growth and development. With Howard on board, I was able to give leadership not only to the doctors and the clinic's board, but I was also able to do this with many other ministries.

I think back on Christ Community Health Services and just sit in awe of what God did and is still doing, how God blessed us even when we made mistakes, and how God brings people to the table who help get the job done. In 1998, the medical clinic needed some expert leadership at the administrative level. The doctors were not only being doctors but also trying to raise funds and administer what was a very cumbersome state reimbursement model. It looked like they would burn out before we reached the kind of scale that had been envisioned. There are just so many hours in a day. They had young families who needed a good portion of those hours as well. We had gone through a few clinic administrators, but none of them worked out. I was in another city with my daughters at the high school state soccer finals and met Burt Waller, the father of one of the other players. We got to talking and I discovered that he was ready to change jobs. He was the president of a local hospital but was leaving his position. He said he was just ready to do something different. I asked him if he would consult with me on the medical ministry and serve as an interim clinic director. Burt came on board and provided both the administrative leadership and the medical business expertise we needed to grow the ministry into what it is today.

MARRS

My wife Becky went back to school to get her master's degree in marriage and family counseling. But before that, she was the director of one of MLF's ministries called MARRS, which stands for Mediation and Restitution/Reconciliation Services, and was established in 1993 in collaboration with Christ United Methodist Church, a church in East Memphis with a heart for the city. Becky and her staff targeted first- or second-time juvenile offenders referred by the juvenile court system in the city. They coached them to meet their victims and make restitution, all the while demonstrating the fact that God was in Christ reconciling the world to himself (2 Corinthians 5:19). MLF created this ministry with the leadership of Don Burford, who had done similar work in California. It was hugely successful and when Don retired, Becky took his place.

For the Kingdom Camp and Retreat Center

During her ministry with MARRS, Becky took some of the MARRS kids to the home of Becky and Eddie Cunningham. The Cunninghams had purchased an estate of over fifty acres that had once belonged to the owners of Stax Records. It had a pool, horse barn, fishing lake, and a huge house. Eddie, a medical doctor, and his wife bought the estate with the dream of making it available to ministry leaders in the city, a place out of the hustle and bustle of the city to come swim, relax, and have fun with the young people God had called them to serve.

We didn't know the Cunninghams at all. We didn't know the estate existed nor did we know about their vision of making it available to others. One summer day, Becky came home and told me about her visits with the kids to this house and meeting with Becky Cunningham. The Cunninghams really wanted to turn their property into a day camp for inner-city kids and wondered if we would meet with them. We did and, ultimately, For the Kingdom Camp and Retreat Center was the result.

God gave the Cunninghams a vision. All MLF did was put wheels on the vision. I can't tell you how many times this has happened. It's so exhilarating to reflect on what God has done, how he orchestrates these divine appointments to get his work done in our city. For the Kingdom Camp and Retreat Center is a beautiful camp for inner-city kids and also serves local churches year-round for weekend retreats, all within the city limits of Memphis. This reduces the cost of transportation to a summer camp for city ministries. When you get to the camp, you soon forget that you are in the city. At first, plans were to build a camp for day use only. There was already a swimming pool, plus tennis and basketball courts. We got volunteers to build some challenge stations like a "faith walk" and a climbing wall in the beautiful woods around the property. The idea was for inner-city youth workers to have a place to take kids for a week, every day, sort of like a sports camp with swimming, good food, and just plain old summer fun. What a gift this was to the city.

Later on as we planned with Eddie and Becky, we wondered why we couldn't build a "full-service" camp, equipped with nice cabins, a bigger swimming pool, a full range of activities, a place where kids could stay the entire week. This way, we would give the urban youth leaders a full camping experience with their young people at a very affordable price.

Getting Kids to Camp

One of the biggest obstacles to camping for urban leaders is the sheer cost of transportation. I remembered how difficult it was for me as a Young Life staffer to get the money together to get kids to camp. Transportation costs on a bus or in vans was just one of the many expenses we had to raise funds for. I always believed in charging the kids something for the camp, even if only a token amount. I have never believed in the sort of ministry that simply "gives" everything away. One of the major pitfalls of food stamps or AFDC is that these programs do not expect any personal responsibility. Empowerment means giving people opportunities so that they can have ownership and maintain dignity. We would put together work projects for the kids to make money if their parents didn't have any to send them to camp. We'd find community projects, like cleaning up vacant lots, as means for kids to earn the fifty bucks they needed to register for camp. This way, the young person had a vested interest in the experience by paying part of his or her own way. We always let the young people know what the full cost of camp was. This way, they also realized that other people cared about them

and were providing scholarships. This way, we could teach
both responsibility and gratitude.

Over time and with a lot of planning, the Cunninghams
decided that building a full-service camp was exactly what
we ought to do. MLF's job was to help put wheels on that
vision, come up with a board of directors, get the camp incorporated with the state and federal agencies, and help raise
some money to get it done. Before long we had the architec-
tural plans, a general contractor, sewer lines dug, electricity
expanded, and everything necessary to build an overnight
facility for up to 150 kids and counselors. This was a huge
undertaking that demanded rezoning from the city council,
all kinds of permits, and a lot of money.

But, again, MLF was making it happen. Through our network of board members and friends we connected with a
local engineering firm that took on the project pro bono. They
got the zoning done and the project was off and running. We
had other sizable donations along the way, too. It's a beautiful
thing to watch God pull it all together, using his people to
get something done in the city. Happens all the time if you
look for it. One way we made this whole thing work was to
get local churches to adopt one cabin and provide labor on
weekends to keep our costs down. Each of the cabins had a
church sponsor. Another local contractor donated the steel
and cranes to build the main building that would house the
kitchen, dining room, and meeting room. We built a huge pool.
Another donor gave us the money to build the Jay Holcomb
Memorial basketball court that was covered so it could be
used in inclement weather. All of this because of a couple who
had a vision from the Lord to create an opportunity for kids to
have fun and hear the gospel. MLF was God's instrument, the
bridge that linked their vision to the finished product.

This is what seeking the peace of the city looks like for

MLF. It looks different in different cities. MLF is all about the theology of place. We are all about being Christ-centered, followers of Jesus and, as such, constantly seeking his will in our city. We like the phrase, "hanging on to Jesus's coattails," meaning we are trying as best we can to follow where Jesus is leading. And he is, you know. In every city, Jesus is doing his work, his way. Our job is to find out where and with whom he is doing his work and to be servant leaders there. And it's often in places we don't suspect, in inner-city neighborhoods with his "little platoons" that are sacrificing everything to expand his kingdom.

Whatcha gonna do?

1. Where is God working in your city?
2. Are you looking for ministries in the heart of your most desperate places?
3. How might you become a 'shalom' seeker in your city?

Chapter 13
How to Heal

*I have often described the near-genocide that white
Europeans inflicted on America's indigenous Native
American peoples and the human bondage forced on kid-
napped Africans as "America's Original Sin."
Today, our sin remains unrepented.*[43]

—Jim Wallis

*To practice journalism in Memphis is to know that lofting
charges of racism is something of a blood sport here. It's a
Memphis version of an improvised explosive device, designed
to inflict harm.*[44]

—Chris Peck, August 5, 2012, in the Memphis *Commercial Appeal*

*In Christ's family there can be no division into Jew
and non-Jew, slave and free, male and female. Among us
you are all equal. That is, we are all in a common
relationship with Jesus Christ.*

—Galatians 3:28-29, MSG

---

43 Jim Wallis, *The Great Awakening: Seven Ways to Change the World* (New
    York: HarperOne, 2009), 162.

44 Chris Peck, "Racism Card Clouds Dialogue," *The Commercial Appeal*,
    August 5, 2012.

There is a photograph in the archives of the Memphis *Commercial Appeal* that features Mayor Henry Loeb standing behind his desk. The photo captures Loeb's stern profile. Facing him is a mass of faces, all Memphis clergy, both black and white, all leaning toward the mayor. The picture was taken on April 5, 1968, the day after Martin Luther King's assassination and two weeks before the end of the sanitation workers' strike.

Loeb's right hand grasps Reverend Joseph P. Toney's. But the mayor's clenched jaw is evidence that the handshake was offered begrudgingly. Rev. Toney's reach covers more than half the distance between the two, although Henry Loeb is by far the larger, taller man. The camera tells the story from the mayor's point of view. Yes, this is a conciliatory meeting, but only on his terms. The shotgun at the ready beneath his desk makes it perfectly clear who has the upper hand.

The upper hand.

No wonder Memphis still has an inferiority complex.

We, white Memphis, had the upper hand for so long and wielded it with so much rank injustice that the rest of Memphis suffered for generations. We are healing now, but we are not completely whole.

LifeFocus '93

In 1993, with Howard on board and MLF growing like crazy, we began to explore the possibilities of developing a structured way to become a healing agent in a Memphis that had languished long and hard under the white man's upper hand. Racial reconciliation got a lot of national press at the time, primarily because of John Perkins' work in Mississippi and the organization he inspired, the Christian Community Development Association. More and more Christian leaders were becoming aware of the impact racism had on both the perpetrator and the victim. Many began to recognize the institutionalized version of racism that was as devastating as the overt kind. Evangelicals finally admitted their silence during the years of slavery, Jim Crow, and the civil rights struggle. It was about time. So MLF brought black and white churches together to create what we called LifeFocus '93, a citywide effort designed to directly confront racism and to empower churches to become agents of racial reconciliation. Because this was such a huge effort, MLF's board "loaned" Howard Eddings to the movement for more than a year, thus giving executive leadership to this transformational event.

We gathered churches across racial barriers that had been as palpable as the wide expanse of Mayor Loeb's desk decades before. The pastors' advisory board that gave leadership to the events was composed of an equal mix of black and white members. More than 100 churches got involved. We started small groups around the issue of racial reconciliation. The results were mixed. Some churches are still connected to this day, while others became disillusioned with the process and gave up. The success stories of LifeFocus '93 are in the relationships that were built.

Many white folks have few, if any, peer relationships with people of different races, particularly baby boomer whites. Far too many see African Americans or Latinos or refugees as "projects." They may give money to a project like tutoring or home ownership. They may even mentor a poor kid, yet they seldom build relationships with black or brown peers that will help them overcome the stereotypes and the racial attitudes they grew up with. The goal of LifeFocus '93 was to change this pattern. Frankly, cultivating friendships with African Americans who have been my peers, mentors, and colleagues has changed my own life. I am far richer as a result.

But there is still much work to be done. Today's young people have a fresh worldview and are far more comfortable with diversity than my generation was and is. But they do not want to be shackled with the past. I often hear comments like these:

"I wasn't even born during the civil rights movement."

"I didn't own slaves."

"I'm not a racist."

This rhetoric does little to heal the institutional racism and white privilege that continues to stack the deck against so many in our cities and our nation. If we do not learn from the past, we'll be sure to repeat it. It's my opinion that this generation must face the reality of the white privilege from which they benefited. Only when they see the poverty and despair our privilege has produced downstream with their own eyes will the current generation develop the will to overcome it.

Healing

Racism is perhaps not as confrontational as it once was in the South, but it still raises its ugly head far too often. KKK rallies still exist, by the way. And the insidious nature of institutional racism will take years to dismantle. Racism is often defined as prejudice plus power. This means that I am in a position or belong to a people group that has the power to make the weight of my prejudice felt. Or racism may be defined as discrimination, based on a belief that my race is superior to another. This type of racism often goes a step further and attributes undesirable and negative traits to a particular race of people. I suppose most blunt racism involves hating other people because of their race and then making the weight of that hatred felt through systematic and institutional discrimination.

Memphis and cities like it have come a long way, but we still have a long way to go. I agree with Jim Wallis, that racism and its history in our country is America's "original sin." The consequences of this sin are scars that will take a long time to heal. But if the church is to be a faithful witness to the reconciliation we have through Jesus, then we must continue to be agents of racial reconciliation. At the heart of racism, of course, is our sin. Racism is a sin, like adultery or idolatry. It's a sin that destroys the racist and victimizes the oppressed. God wants to give us a new heart and new eyes. He created each of us in his image and to reject that image in another human being is the height of arrogance and pride. This is why my friend Eli Morris says, "Racism is spitting in the face of God." Racism flat out denies that God created humanity in his own image.

I have been on a number of panels about racial prejudice. Often, I start such a panel or lecture with the admission that I am a "recovering racist." People generally take issue with this statement. But it's true. I believe that you cannot grow up as a white male in a segregated nation and not feel superior to every other race in the world. And, I might add, superior to women, too. That is simply the culture in which I was raised. Even though I don't remember any racial slurs used in our home, the surrounding culture was thoroughly racist. It was "just the way things were," as if racism was justifiable due to cultural norms. African American men were called boys. My parents, like many middle-class families in the South, had an African American "maid" who cleaned the house, washed clothes, and so forth. I don't remember any of their last names. We called them by their first names, although we always were taught to address white adult men and women using Mr., Mrs., or Miss before their last names. It was hard to not see the superiority of the white race as a kid growing up in the '50s or '60s. I didn't even know African American doctors, lawyers, and architects existed. I just assumed all African Americans worked for white people or had other menial jobs.

Even the more "enlightened" whites had this sense of their own superiority. I remember several of my friends' parents who were on the "right side" of the civil rights struggle as white people. They were vocal advocates for integration. Yet they, too, often belonged to exclusive country clubs that did not allow black membership or in some cases didn't allow Jewish membership, either. They, too, had "maids" they addressed by their first names. These more enlightened folks were paternalistic. They essentially treated African Americans as their children who couldn't take care of themselves. No, the culture I grew up in was racist through and through. I am still recovering from decades of racist indoctrination. The scars run deep.

Confession

I often stress in these seminars or panels that the first step to being freed from sin is confession. I must look myself in the mirror and confess that I was raised to be superior and to treat African American, Latinos, Asians, and Native Americans as my inferiors. We were taught that blacks were lazy and sex-crazed animals, that Latinos were thieves and always dirty, and that Native Americans were drunken savages. No one sat us down, mind you, and taught us this, but it was the message of our culture, loud and clear. So I take ownership of that ugliness and confess it. I admit that I am a racist, that I am prideful, and that I believe myself to be superior based on nothing other than white privilege.

Then I confess that I have benefited from white privilege; white upper middle-class privilege at that. There was never any doubt that I'd go to college, even though my dad was the only one in his family who did. It was a settled fact that I'd never be hungry. I would be able to do whatever it was I set out to do. This was my firm belief, and I daresay it was one shared by many peers as well. Even whites who were not middle class were considered superior to people of color. This is deeply ingrained in my psyche, as it is for so many of my generation if they will but think it through.

I was asked to speak to a young adult Sunday school class at an affluent church in Memphis a few years ago about racial reconciliation. I gladly accepted. I started as I often do with my confession, "I am a recovering racist." This was not well accepted. "I'm not a racist," person after person said. "I've never discriminated against anyone due to race," another said. "Some of my best friends are black," still another one retorted. I'm used to this, so I pressed on. Everyone in the class owned a home, at least one nice car, and had a college or even graduate education. Most had attended private prep schools that were second to none. All had middle-class or wealthy parents. Talk about white privilege! But they refused to see how the deck was stacked in their favor from the womb, and how it was stacked against people of color. I stuck to my guns then and I still do. I had privileges based on nothing other than the fact that I was born white.

Repentance

If we confess our sins, "He is faithful and just to forgive us our sins and cleanse us from all unrighteousness." (1 John 1:9) It's one thing to confess our sins to the Lord, but that isn't all there is. The essential next step is repentance, which means going in the opposite direction from the sin I confess. John did not mean we were to keep on sinning, confessing, go back to sinning, and so on. The Lord wants to change our hearts and our minds. We are each temples of the Holy Spirit and we are to grow more and more into the likeness of Jesus Christ through the power of the indwelling Holy Spirit. So after I confess my racism, I must then look for ways to repent.

But what does that look like? First, it means to immerse myself in the racial group that has been wronged by my sinful attitudes. I must educate myself about their culture. I started this process in high school by reading the works of Martin Luther King Jr., Malcolm X, Richard Wright, W.E. Dubois, and others. I read *Before the Mayflower: A History of Black America*. I read theology written by African American, African, Native American, and Latino scholars. One of the greatest educational experiences in our city is the National Civil Rights Museum. It is a wonderful gift to our city and the world. I am surprised at how many of my fellow Memphians have never visited the museum. (So here's a shameless plug: It is located at the Lorraine Motel where Dr. King was assassinated. Go find it.)

But there is another aspect of education, one that takes me beyond theory into reality. I must expose myself to the culture that I have wronged. That's why I started volunteering as a college student. That's a big reason behind the Urban Plunge we do with Hope Presbyterian every year. We want people who have perhaps never been to the "hood" to experience it firsthand.

Compassionate Relationships

Without deep, honest relationships with people who don't look like me, racial reconciliation is simply an intellectual exercise. Relationships are key. This is where honest dialogue can really take place, and where my heart can be truly transformed.

The scriptures give us a clear model for the kinds of relationships we are to build with people, especially with hurting, oppressed people. Hebrews 4:12 describes Jesus as a great High Priest who sympathizes with our weaknesses. The Greek word for sympathy here is *sumpatheo*, and it means to suffer with, to enter into "patheo" or pathos with the other. The Incarnation was for Jesus a guaranteed journey into our pathos.

The ministry of presence and place I mentioned in earlier chapters is rooted in this idea. Yes, the gospels tell us Jesus was often "filled with compassion" (in John 11:32, Mark 1:32, and Matthew 15:32, to name a few places), but what engendered that compassion? The Incarnation. Because Jesus was present in our world, he now sees us as neighbors, as friends, and not projects. We are not "those people" over there, but we are related to him as intimately as possible. Because Jesus sees us up close and personal as one of us, he is compassionate toward us.

Seeing people the way Jesus sees them is the beginning of compassion. We can go an entire lifetime without really seeing people and situations as Jesus sees them. Seeing is a choice. For example, the early Jewish Christians who were gathered in and around Jerusalem still considered Gentiles as dogs. It took a vision from the Lord to recalibrate Peter's vision, to reveal to him that all people were created in God's image, just like he was. How do we see? Do we see the homeless guy as nothing more than a bum or a drug addict? How does Jesus see him? Our sin, our own fallenness, and our culture prevent us from seeing clearly the way God sees. We see with sinful eyes through the lens of our culture, our background, or perhaps our wealth.

We are all sinners, all guilty before a holy God. This means none of us can presume to adopt a judgmental attitude toward anyone else. Our salvation was not our own doing but was a matter of God's grace. We are forgiven people, and because we are forgiven, we can perceive others as Jesus did, as people for whom he died, people he desperately loves. All people are created in God's image for his pleasure. *All* people.

The response of God's heart to what he sees in us is

compassion. The Greek translation for this word is rather graphic. The word *splanchonxna* is akin to *sumpatheo*. It means entering into and identifying with the pathos of the other so completely that one is "deeply moved," way down inside. Unfortunately, some versions of the Bible translate *splanchonxna* as the word "pity," but that's not the meaning of the word. Pity means feeling sorry for someone. Compassion is not the same as pity or sentimentality. The word *splanchonxna* means being moved in the gut, in the bowels. It is deep identification with people who are in pain or need.

In many of the "compassion texts" in the gospels, Jesus not only sees and feels compassion for a person with a particular need, but he acts in order to meet that need. In the same way, the ministry of compassion is not only about seeing people as Jesus sees them. It is about taking action as a result of what we see. Like Jesus at the tomb of Lazarus, we may weep with those who hurt, but if at all possible, we'll act to ease that hurt.

When I lived outside of the community in my Young Life days in Orange Mound, I didn't really understand the people who lived there. They weren't yet my neighbors. They would tell me about police brutality or about streetlights not working and nothing being done about it. They would tell me about the lack of health services or absentee slumlords charging too much rent. But I couldn't fully see or feel their pain because it wasn't my pain. But when I began to practice the ministry of presence or the theology of place, when I became a member of the community, a real neighbor, then their problems became my problems. We *see* differently when we practice presence. We practice *sumpatheo*. So when we see the mistreatment of our neighbors, it's no longer them, it's us. When your *neighbor* experiences police brutality (in the 1970s the vast majority of MPD officers were white and racism was rampant in the force), it's very different from hearing about it on the radio or the five o'clock news.

Compassion is the prevailing attitude God has toward us. He so loved the world that he gave his only Son. While we were yet sinners and his enemies, Christ died for us, the just for the unjust. He who knew no sin became sin on our behalf, that we might become the righteousness of God in him. Compassion is at the very heart of God. God is love, but his love translates into concrete action. Jesus entered our world, into our pathos and he *"sumpatheoed"* with us. Compassion is the kind of love that leads to action on behalf of others.

Ripping Off the Band-Aid

These steps of confession, repentance, education, and building compassionate relationships can be pursued by individuals who grew up in our cities, especially the Southern cities with histories like the one still evolving in Memphis. But this is a corporate issue as much as an individual one, and it calls for corporate action as well. I cannot confess sins for others, but I can certainly confess my own in the context of community and hope to bring others along in the process.

Through MLF and other churches and organizations, we're experiencing healing year by year in Memphis. One vehicle of healing for the past twenty years has been the Urban Plunge. It's just what it sounds like: an intentional immersion in the city. And it's pretty intense. During orientation, one of the leaders has been known to say, "I'm gonna rip the Band-Aid off your soul!"[45]

Maybe that's just what it takes to bring about authentic healing. In the Urban Plunge we take a group from Hope Presbyterian Church and spend Thursday through Sunday in the inner city, visiting ministries, doing a service project, teaching the group about the importance of justice, God's concern for the city, and the importance of facing our own

---

45 Pastor Rudy Howard.

racial prejudices. I've participated in the Urban Plunge twice every year for twenty years. Other churches in Memphis and other cities have done similar projects. Urban Plunge not only educates people about the city and exposes them to it in different ways; it helps them see it with new eyes. At its best, it launches new relationships that continue after the long weekend is over.

One participant had this to say at the end of his Urban Plunge: "I've been so unaware of what's going on in my own city. It's just eye-opening, and I know it's going to be life-changing. It's really different to be standing here and feeling like you're doing something meaningful instead of just driving through."[46] Another saw reason to hope:

> We all saw for ourselves that the needs in the inner city for godly people are many. But we also saw the fact that godly people are already there and good work is already being done. The enemy and lawlessness once ruled those areas, now there's definitely a new sheriff in town and his name is Jesus.[47]

The desk with the gun beneath it in Mayor Henry Loeb's office represented an unspoken, imposing, and dangerous dividing line between human beings that was predicated upon nothing more than the colors of their skin.

I began this book with an assumption about you: that you love the city, your city. That the dividing lines that existed decades ago still exist today, perhaps in different iterations, and dishearten you and maybe even make you mad. That's good. But not good enough. Discouragement and anger alone are not enough to fuel love. The history of the city cannot

---

46   http://www.gabaptist.org/FAITHNETWORK_USERFILESTORE/file-cabinet/ministries/237e6518-ae1d-4db3-844a-2959aa6966fc/research_services/rs_efc_the_urban_plunge.pdf

47   Ibid.

propel you to redemptive action unless you begin to see yourself in that history: to take ownership, to some extent, of the basic evils of that history. And to take the journey, as I did forty years ago, from a ministry more affected by racism than I wanted to admit, to an urban love affair.

Back in 1968, the barrier to love between races—between people—was as concrete as Mayor Loeb's desk and his gun. Today, it is nearly invisible. Not non-existent, but much harder to see.

But Jesus sees it. And because he sees it, I believe I am responsible to see it, too. I must not only see it, I must do all I can to eradicate it. Because that's the only way to really love the city.

Whatcha gonna do?

1. As you examine your own heart, culture, heritage, etc., from what do you need to repent? What positive steps can you take toward repentance that will move you in a different direction?
2. If you're white and reading this book, do you recoil at the idea of white privilege? How has being white stacked the deck in your favor? Or has it?
3. Compassion: Is it paternalism or genuine gut-wrenching compassion that leads to action? How has charity become toxic to you rather than redemptive and life giving? Do you write a check to ministries that serve the poor and be done with it or do you engage in the lives of those on the margins of society?
4. What is your worldview? How do you view poverty? Is it the result of folks making bad choices? Or is it something more?
5. How will you engage your city?

Postscript
By Dr. John M. Perkins

In a society where many believe racism is over and our past should be forgotten, Larry Lloyd's book, *Recovering from Racism,* comes at the right time. Larry has given us a necessary, historical overview of his own life and the times in which he grew up, that is still very relevant to the world we find ourselves in today. I was also living during the time Larry is talking about in this book, and though it may seem far away from where we are now, it is still offering something we all need to reflect on.

As we look around, there seems to be a new movement in the church, particularly among young Evangelicals, to start asking the question "What is justice?" again. But this time, they are doing it with an understanding that all people were created equal and in the image of God. As a result, this new emerging generation is engaged in planting and establishing multicultural churches and ministries in neighborhoods of need all over the world. Many of the principles that are evident both in *Recovering from Racism* and in Larry's life are relevant and important for this new generation of enthusiastic young people seeking to bring this vision of a truly diverse church into reality.

In 2 Chronicles 7:14 we are told, "If my people, who are called by my name, will humble themselves and pray and seek my face and turn from their wicked ways, then I will hear from heaven, and I will forgive their sin and will heal their land." While it is easy to forget the past and the sins of yesterday, this young generation needs to come to know the depths of the sin of racism. It is hard for many people to fully grasp, but if we don't know the full wickedness of racism and bigotry, then we are not able to offer a repentance that truly says we are sorry for our sin. As a result, both blacks and whites, as well as those across the world affected by other forms of racism, are left deeply damaged and unable to fully be freed from the sins of the past.

Part of that damage is the guilt many white folks feel regarding their privilege, and the blame we black folk are willing to put on them. This constant problem of blaming and guilt and understanding privilege is something that we don't know how to deal with today. Larry's book speaks to this problem, but also gives people a better understanding of what to do with their guilt and privilege. Larry Lloyd, himself has had a lot of privilege, getting a good education, going to premiere schools like Rhodes College and Fuller Seminary, and even obtaining a Doctorate degree. Larry's skills, economic savvy, and biblical training gave him a solid foundation to train new leaders in Young Life and ultimately organize the resources for an institution that could provide sustainable community development anchored in the local church and business community.

But it was his relocation back home to the urban community of Memphis that really gets at a proper response to white guilt and privilege. In his relocation, Larry was able to build deep friendships and relationships in a way that was genuine instead of paternalistic. Larry has a great ability to learn from others, both black and white, and the outcome is what you see laid out in this book. As one of my favorite poems says:

Go to the people

Live among them
Learn from them
Love them
Start with what they know
Build on what they have.
But of the best leaders
When their task is accomplished
Their work is done
The people will remark,
"We have done it ourselves."

The example Larry provides of the work he did after discovering his privilege is extremely helpful and gives us a lens through which we can look at our past while simultaneously looking inside of ourselves in order to offer the real repentance we need in response to the deep sin we have committed in the racism and injustices of our society. The verse I quoted earlier from 2 Chronicles is speaking to our privilege, to our blindness, and our inability to turn away from our sin. But it is when we turn, repent, and humble ourselves that God says he will heal our land. I see Larry's life and this book as a big part of our healing process.

From the time Larry was in California until now, we have worked together. We have enjoyed a deep friendship, and I thank God that I have been a part of his life. I'm going to use this book in the rest of my life's ministry and I'm going to pass it on to others who could learn much from his life experience. Read this book, absorb this book, and be changed by it.

—Dr. John M. Perkins
Co-founder of the Christian Community Development Association (CCDA)
Co-founder of Christian Community Health Fellowship
Founder and President Emeritus of the John and Vera Mae Perkins
Foundation

Acknowledgments

I am deeply grateful to Mrs. Kitti Murray who collaborated with me on the early drafts. She is a gifted writer and is involved in her own ministry in the Atlanta area. Thanks to Thonda Barnes for her help on designing the cover for this book.

I am indebted to the Memphis Leadership Foundation and Hope Christian Community Foundation...their boards, staff and the thousands of people who give so many hours to ministry in the heart of our city through the various ministries that we serve.

My mentors: Fred Davis, Verley Sangster and William Pannell have given me so much guidance over the last 40 years. I can't imagine not having mentors in my life. John Perkins refuses to let me call him my mentor, preferring the term colleague...but whatever...he's been a mentor to me regardless.

Howard Eddings has been my partner in ministry in one way or another for over 30 years. When people meet me, they think I'm Howard and vice versa. On almost every issue, we think along similar paths. Pretty scary! Our work together and friendship is particularly special.

And I am most grateful for my family: wife Becky since 1975 who has been on my case to get this book finally published that I started five years ago; my four wonderful daughters, Leah, Lydia, Charis and Hannah, sons-in-laws and five grandchildren (so far!).

I love my city. I hope by reading this book, you will grow to love yours. God's at work in your city. Find out where and get on board!

—Larry Lloyd

183